UPFRONT

and

STRAIGHTFORWARD

Let the Manipulative Game Players Know What You're REALLY Thinking

Alan Roger Currie

Mode One Multimedia, Inc.
USA

Printed in the United States of America.

Mode One Enterprises, Inc.
2009

Other books by Alan Roger Currie:

Mode One: Let the Women Know What You're REALLY Thinking

http://www.modeone.net

UPFRONT

and

STRAIGHTFORWARD

Let the Manipulative Game Players Know What You're REALLY Thinking

Alan Roger Currie

ACKNOWLEDGMENTS

May God Bless the Spirits of my late father, Clarence R. Currie, and my late my mother, Mildred R. Currie; Much love always to my brother and ace confidante, Stephen C. Currie; Cousins Atha Baugh, Christopher Currie and Jason P. Jones; my close friends Timothy Beverly, DeMarrio Gray, Jeff Kenton, Ervin V. Pulliam III, Cory Pulliman and Maurice L. Taylor.

Others: Lisa DeNeal, Garrard McClendon, Adrienne Yates, Keith Olivetti, Michael Bennett, Anthrice Bray, Kimberly J. Brown, Wendy English, Chi Blackburn, Armand Carr, Gordon Chube, Jeri Goosby-Smith, Greg Hines, Kimberly Jones-Snipe, Wendy Kinkead, John Leslie, Carleton Lewis, Walt "Baby" Love, Demetria Lucas, Theo McClendon, Angelique Perrin, Philip R. Pulliam, Toni Reed, John Soo Hoo, Anthony Spinelli, Greg Tufaro, Anthony Walker, Wilton Waverly, Steve "The Dean" Williams, Felix Willis, Andrea Wilson and Nikki Woods.

Much thanks to many of the fellow authors, attraction and seduction experts, dating coaches, relationships advisors, and other professional colleagues who I truly admire and have had the opportunity to interact with, interview, and exchange ideas with. I'm not going to list specific names, but you know who you are. Special kudos to the fellas at Direct-Method.com

To all of the women who I have dated, been intimate with, engaged in confidential and/or provocative conversations with, and even those who we experienced some degree of animosity and/or contentious interactions . . . I've learned a lot about myself as a result of knowing you, and I have gained a lot of knowledge and wisdom about the opposite gender. Thank you.

CONTENTS

Chapter ONE

Mode One – Feedback and Fallout

Who would have thought that when I wrote down The Four Modes of Verbal Communication™ on a napkin back in October 1990 that the whole "Mode One" phenomenon would have become an international sensation. Since the paperback version was published in late February of 2006, I have received requests to have *Mode One: Let the Women Know What You're REALLY Thinking* translated into Chinese, French, German, Japanese, Portuguese, and Spanish.

Because of the popularity of both the Ebook and paperback versions of *Mode One*, I now receive Email messages and requests for personal consultations from men and women who not only reside in cities throughout the United States, but who live in a number of different countries all over the globe.

The primary demographic group I targeted with *Mode One* were single, heterosexual men who were **a)** afraid to approach women in general; **b)** confident enough to approach women, but had the tendency to engage in too much trivial, inconsequential "small talk"; **c)** frequently making the mistake of confusing women who are erotically uninhibited and/or promiscuous with women who were prudish and very monogamous-minded; and finally **d)** suffering from a high degree of misogynistic bitterness towards the female gender as a whole as the result of years of perceiving women as being unfair to them and/or disrespectful to them.

When I first had *Mode One* published, it was my prediction that approximately 99% of the men who read it would give it an enthusiastic "thumbs up," and maybe 40-50% of the women who read it would feel the same way. Well, to my surprise, probably 80-90% of the women who have read my book enjoyed it as much as the men.

Women read my book for primarily two reasons: **1)** To simply better understand how the minds of men work, and what are the desires and motivations for approaching women in the first place; **2)** To see what type of manipulative head games men employ with women.

Without question, the #1 challenge and criticism to my book from both men and women was the assertion that, *"you can't just walk up to a woman and let her know you only want to have casual sex with her. That is rude, disrespectful, shallow, socially inappropriate, and just plain tacky."*

I can think of a few more minor, nitpicky criticisms of *Mode One*, but generally, the vast majority of the criticisms I received were directly or indirectly related to the idea that Mode One Behavior was representative of behavior that is perceived as "too forward," "too blunt" and/or "too sexually straightforward and provocative."

At the risk of being perceived as cocky, I will let it be known that I broke down a lot of women who attempted to challenge me about my Mode One principles and philosophies. I'm speaking of women with Masters degrees, PhDs, J.D.s, and any other highly educated degree you can think of. I didn't break them down with any complicated, profound intelligence, but rather simple logic and basic questions.

My main argument was, and still is, why would ANY WOMAN want a man to lie to her ... or 'trick' her ... into having casual sex with him? Wouldn't any woman want to be given the choice of whether or not to reciprocate a man's desire and interest in casual sex?

I had some factions suggest that my book was "not Christian-like." Is not being straightforwardly honest about your true desires, interests and intentions a part of being a devout Christian? And besides ... who said *Mode One* was exclusively for Christians? I want those who are atheists and agnostic to read my book too.

Here is/was the biggest "misconception" about *Mode One*: Mode One is a book that promotes the idea of casual sex as a higher priority than being involved in a long-term, monogamous romantic relationship. This is where a lot of women (and even a few men) misinterpreted my book. *Mode One* basically says to men, if you know for a 100% fact that your interest is exclusively casual sex, why not just be upfront and straightforward about it?

Then, a startling revelation kept being pounded into my mind. Believe it or not, there are many women who **want** men to be misleading and deceitful about their desire for one-night stands, weekend flings, and other variations of non-monogamous casual sex.

"What?!? That can't be!" you say. *"That makes no sense. What woman in her right mind would WANT a man to pretend like he wants a long-term relationship, when in reality, he only wants casual sex?? That woman would have to be stupid or crazy!!"* She is neither. Instead, she is cunning, calculating and manipulative. I will discuss the manipulative tactics employed by many women in more detail in Chapter Three, Chapter Four, Chapter Seven and Chapter Eight.

If you are a man or woman who absolutely despises manipulative head games, then you are a fan and supporter of Mode One Behavior; If you are a man or woman who feels like you generally tend to benefit from lying to the opposite sex, misleading the opposite sex, and/or engaging in head games with the opposite sex, then nine times out of ten, you're going to be a harsh critic of the principles and philosophies outlined in my previous *Mode One* book.

If you are a man or woman who likes to fancy yourself a member of the former group, but deep-down, you are really in the latter group, you might as well sell this copy of your book on eBay. This book is not for you. This book is for people who have no desire to repeatedly engage in manipulative game-playing. If you are truly in this group, please . . . continue to read on.

As I did in my previous book, *Mode One: Let the Women Know What You're REALLY Thinking*, at the end of each chapter I always tend to ask a handful of interesting questions to get you to be totally truthful **with yourself** regarding your true desires, motivations, interests, and intentions as it relates to dating and relationships.

Questions:

1) Do you own an Ebook copy or paperback copy of *Mode One: Let the Women Know What You're REALLY Thinking*? How would you evaluate the effectiveness of your own interpersonal communication as it relates to conversing with members of the opposite sex?

2) Do you sometimes prefer "pleasant lies" over raw, real truth?

<u>Quick Note</u>: After ***Mode One: Let the Women Know What You're REALLY Thinking*** was published, many readers suggested that I repeated many of my themes, principles, and philosophies almost ad nauseam. Trust me folks: that was INTENTIONAL.

What I've noticed from many men and women who read ***Mode One*** is that **some people read what they want to read**. They don't read what you've actually written, but rather, what they THINK you have written. Some people just browse through a number of pages in the various chapters looking for the most significant hints, tips, tidbits and the most helpful pieces of advice instead of reading the book thoroughly. Consequently, much of the content of my book ends up getting misinterpreted and/or taken out of context.

Therefore, in my discussions about **manipulative head games**, you are going to find me reiterating many points over and over and over again. This is my writing style (along with sometimes unwarranted **bold** text, CAPITALIZED text, *italicized* text, "quoted" text, and <u>underlined</u> text). Get used to it. My writing style is what it is.

Chapter TWO

Traditional Dating
VS
21st Century Dating

What exactly is **dating**? Many men and women use the term "dating" very loosely, and even to a certain extent, inappropriately. For example, many men and women believe that if a man and a woman are involved in a monogamous romantic relationship, this means that they are "dating." Actually, this is somewhat of a misnomer.

Dating is to being in a relationship what shopping for clothes is to actually purchasing clothes. Based on what I would refer to as "traditional" or "old school" philosophies towards what the term 'dating' means, I will go with this definition: To say that a person is dating means that this man or woman is in regular communication with a single, unattached member of the opposite sex, and this person is hanging out socially with a number of different members of the opposite sex to determine who is the most compatible candidate to be involved in a steady, exclusively committed relationship (Gay men and Lesbian women not included in this discussion).

For example, if over the last 12-16 months, I've only been in communication with one woman ... and I've spent all of my free time with one woman ... then I am not really "dating" that woman. I'm essentially in a relationship with her, even if we have never referred to each other as "boyfriend" and "girlfriend."

When you are truly dating, you are going out with a wide variety of men or women to identify similar interests, tolerable differences and intolerable differences. Using the shopping analogy again, it would be like me trying on eight or nine different double-breasted suits before I decide on the one double-breasted suit that I am going to purchase. Again, this was the basic concept of dating from those who are a part of my late mother and father's generation.

This is why most men and women from my parents' generation frowned on the idea of premarital sex and/or casual sex. Because once you start having sex with someone, you might as well be in a steady relationship with them. You see, no one would frown on a man going out with a new and different woman every other night over a two or three month period if he were not engaged in sexual activity with those women. Many who possess the "old school" mindset would simply say, "Oh, he's just **dating**." In the 1930s, 40s, and 50s, that's generally what it meant when you said someone was "dating."

There is a popular show on syndicated television entitled *elimiDate*. You have one guy, who starts out the night with four women, and by the end of the episode, he ends up with one woman (or sometimes, it's flipped where you will have one woman at the beginning of the episode with four men).

elimiDate is a great example of how the old school concept of dating worked. A man would start off with say, six women ... then he would socialize with those six women until he began to narrow that number down to five women, then four, then three, then two. . . and then finally, he decided on the one "special woman" with whom he wanted to go steady with. Sound simple and structured enough? Cool.

Side Note: When I resided in Los Angeles, I was involved with a very popular "megachurch" that would encourage dating in the "old school" manner; the leaders of the church would encourage the men to go out on a date every week with a different sister in the church.

Then, the brothers in the church would select maybe five to ten sisters to go out on a second date with; from there, a slightly lesser number of sisters to go out on a third and fourth date with, until ultimately, the brother in the church selected the one sister who he wanted to be his steady girlfriend. Given that no sexual activity was allowed, that concept actually worked, and worked very well.

For the most part, dating in that manner has virtually disappeared in contemporary society. Today, I believe dating is far more complicated, confusing, challenging and frustrating for many single men and women attempting to find "the one" (i.e., their romantic "soulmate"). Welcome to 21st Century dating for singles.

As I alluded to already, what made the "old school" manner of dating work were the low occurrences of premarital sex and/or casual sex. Once men and women started having sex before marriage, and even more so, sex outside the context of a steady, exclusively committed relationship, the entire dynamic of dating was changed **forever**.

I believe this change first started taking place during the era of the "Sexual Revolution" and "Free Love" phenomenon in the 1960s and 70s. During this two-decade period, there was a significant change from old school dating to "new school dating." Once women got comfortable with birth control pills and other birth control methods, and men got increasingly comfortable with condoms, the instances of premarital sex and casual sex exploded.

The end result of that transition from one form of conservative dating rituals to a more open and free-spirited form of dating is that engaging in sexual activity is no longer exclusively associated with the idea of getting married like it was in my parents' generation.

We now live in an age where even pre-teens in middle school are having orgies and blowjob parties on their lunch hour, or afterschool (no joke; this has been highlighted in magazine articles and on morning television talk shows). There are men today who are teenagers or in their twenties who don't even believe in the idea of a monogamous relationship. They can't even relate to that concept.

Many young men today believe in having a "harem." Some of these young womanizers refer to the women in their lives as "their stable of hos (whores)." STDs are being passed around like crazy these days. Bi-sexual men are passing on the HIV virus to their girlfriends and wives. The term "men on the down low" is a common phrase.

Make no mistake . . . it's not just the men in society today who are promiscuous and out of control. Women today are far more erotically uninhibited and promiscuous than women in the first half of the Twentieth Century. Women want to enjoy the lustful pleasures of multiple sex partners just as much, if not more, than most men do.

This directly relates to why there are so many manipulative head games being employed between men and women these days. I believe manipulative game-playing is more rampant than ever before. One of the main reasons why you have so many manipulative head games being employed in today's dating scene is because you have a lot of men and women who are sexually duplicitous and erotically hypocritical walking around pretending as though they are 'innocent,' 'virtuous,' and erotically conservative and only into monogamous relationships ... when in reality, they love kinky sex and promiscuous sex as much as any currently employed adult film star does.

Think about it: Hypothetically, if all men and women in society were divided into two groups ... those men and women who only have an interest in a long-term, monogamous relationship ... and those men and women who are only enthused about engaging in casual, non-monogamous sex ... finding a romantic companion and/or sexual lover would be a fairly easy and straightforward process.

What makes dating and relationships far more complicated and frustrating than it really needs to be is the fact that you have men and women who are 'pretending' to be interested in only monogamous relationships, when in reality, they really want to enjoy sexual pleasure with a variety of new and different partners.

The second major contributor to the increase of manipulative game-playing is that you have women who want to be offered "incentives" and "rewards" in exchange for their romantic and/or sexual companionship. I discussed this in Chapter Two of *Mode One*. You have men who are more-than-willing to offer these women their desired incentives and rewards. Let the head games commence.

There are pretty much only six relationships a man and a woman (who are not blood related) can have with each other:

1) A long-term, monogamous sexual relationship
(e.g., husband & wife)

2) A long-term, non-monogamous sexual relationship
(e.g., "friends with benefits" or "fuck buddies")

3) A short-term, monogamous sexual relationship
(e.g., your normal short lived "boyfriend-girlfriend" relationship that doesn't have a chance of leading to marriage)

4) A short-term, non-monogamous sexual relationship
(e.g., a one-night stand, weekend fling, etc)

5) A long-term, non-sexual, platonic relationship
(e.g., high school or college classmate, long-time co-worker, etc)

6) A short-term, non-sexual, platonic relationship
(e.g., casual acquaintances, brief co-workers, brief neighbors, etc)

If every man and woman who was interested in a relationship that falls into Category #1 were to express their interests upfront and straightforwardly, there would be no manipulative head games needed. Same with Categories #2 thru #6.

The reality is some people who want a relationship in Category #2 will pretend as though they are searching for a relationship in Category #1; Some people who want a relationship in Category #4 will pretend to want a relationship in Category #3 or #6. And so on, and so on. This is the primary basis behind head games. Head games begin when your fear of rejection becomes so overwhelming, to the point where you just can't fathom not having your way. You want the response, reaction and result you desire so badly that you will do anything to achieve it.

For men, Mode One Behavior is the most effective means of identifying when a woman is not being totally genuine about her desires, interests and intentions. For women, being upfront and straightforward with their romantic and/or sexual desires and interests is beneficial as well, but there is usually more required on their part.

My early advice to women: Do not engage in premarital sex and/or casual sex if you do not have the emotional fortitude to deal with the potential consequences or repercussions. I have had conversations with too many women who think single men should operate with a "code of ethics" when it comes to casual sex. Casual sex is casual sex. There are no established rules or obligations to exhibit integrity.

That is the difference between a married relationship and an unmarried relationship. A married relationship is based on predetermined spiritual and legal rules, guidelines, boundaries, and values. When you engage in sexual relations with someone who is not your husband or wife, you are entering into that relationship based on your own desires and expectations for how you want that relationship to work out. Sort of like jumping into a swimming pool with that "Swim at Your Own Risk" sign and no lifeguard nearby.

I've had friends and acquaintances view writing a book about dating and relationships as "trivial." Dating is an important part of our life. Let's be real folks: The first thing that determines the quality of your upbringing as a child is the relationship between your mother and father. You are alive right now because of love, lust or sexual abuse.

If you were born as a product of a loving, caring relationship between your mother and father, feel BLESSED. Nine times out of ten, you received a lot of love from both of your parents, and your upbringing was probably not filled with too much "drama" or animosity between your mother and father.

On the other hand, if your mother and father had a contentious relationship . . . before, during or after you were born . . . whether you want to acknowledge it or not, this inevitably had to have an adverse affect on your upbringing.

If you were brought up by a mother who harbors bitterness and resentment towards the men who she feels "dogged her out" or physically and/or emotionally abused her, there is a good chance that you're going to grow up around negative attitudes being espoused towards men.

If you were brought up by a father who had a gold digger or highly promiscuous whore-type as a girlfriend or temporary wife, then you're going to view women quite differently than most of your friends who come from an emotionally stable, two-parent household.

Make no mistake: Romantic and sexual relationships contribute to the quality of our life just as much as clean air, money, good health and quality friends do. Discussing and analyzing people's dating habits and rituals is by no means "trivial."

I really don't consider myself a dating expert or a relationship expert. When I've been interviewed on radio and/or television, I'm often referred to as a relationship expert, but in reality, that is not a valid title. It is very flattering … but again, it is not altogether valid.

I'm simply a man who has a keen sense of observation of other human beings' habits, behavioral nuances, interpersonal communication tendencies, and body language signals. At the time I write this book, there is a very popular television show on the CBS network entitled, *The Mentalist.*

A "mentalist" is not really a psychic, but rather he or she is a person who studies people's habits, nuances, tendencies and body language signs to the point where he or she can predict what the person who they are observing is going to do next and/or what the person who is being observed has already done.

I've had many friends of mine over the years suggest that I possess a talent of perception and observation that would informally qualify me as a dating and relationships "mentalist." I choose real world observation over academic research when it comes to drawing conclusions about dating.

I can name many instances where I have predicted a couple was going to break up or get divorced weeks, months or even years before the couple involved even had a clue that something was wrong in their relationship. I constantly study the nuances of the opposite gender as

17

well as the nuances of my own gender with a particular emphasis on their interpersonal communication habits. I watch this very, very **closely**. I study how men and women communicate their desires and interests to one another.

I have a natural knack for identifying phony, disingenuous, manipulative type men and women from real, honest, non-manipulative type men and women within a brief time period of interaction and observation.

Usually, within the first five-to-ten minutes of a conversation with a person, I can quickly assess if a person **a)** is prudish or kinky; **b)** is materialistic or non-materialistic; **c)** hangs around people with high moral character and integrity or low character and integrity; **d)** frequently lies to people or tells others the truth; and **e)** gets what they want by straightforwardly asking for it, or do they try to 'sneak through the back door' to get what they want.

So it is this characteristic of mine ... or talent of mine ... that makes me SEEM to others who meet me that I am some sort of "relationship expert," but the reality is, **I am just really, really good and sizing up various behavioral attributes in people in a short period of time**.

<u>Side note</u>: If you watch one of the episodes from the first season of **Californication** starring former X-Files standout David Duchovny, his character (Hank Moody) once did this while at dinner with friends. Hank met this woman (who his friends were trying to set him up with), and then after only about five or ten minutes of conversation, he told her what type of woman she was, what type of men she had dated, and what her most recent dating experiences had been like. The woman's face became so serious, and later tense, that you could just surmise the vast majority of his perceptions were on point. She became so frustrated that she just got up and walked out.

I don't usually do what Hank Moody did with women I meet in the first conversation, but I've done that many times in the second, third or fourth conversation. I've actually had many women say, *"Wow. Alan, that was impressive. I almost feel like you have my past [dating] life on video somewhere. I can't believe so many of your assessments about me were so valid and on-point!"*

I am particularly perceptive with women who are "**undercover freaks**" (i.e., Urban slang for "Wholesome Pretenders" which I explained and described in **Mode One**; Women who publicly try to give you the impression that they are "innocent" and "wholesome," but are really very free-spirited sexually and erotically uninhibited, and to one degree or another, promiscuous).

A lot of men and women have this naïve notion that all men behave in the same manner towards all women and vice versa, and this is such a wrong conclusion. I have observed a woman behave like a church-going, monogamous-minded, semi-prudish "good girl" with one group of men, and then turn around and behave like the most open-minded, free-spirited, semi-promiscuous "kinky freak" type with a different group of men. Studying sexual duplicity is a specialty of mine. I am fascinated by how duplicitous and/or hypocritical many men and women are in regard to their own sexuality.

When I meet women who are involved in a long-term relationship, I can usually tell within ten-to-fifteen minutes (or less) after being in her presence if that woman is cheating on her boyfriend, fiancé, or husband even before her male companion has any inkling or clue of it.

The very first thing I study with women is their eyes. This is why my own eyes are on the cover of both of my books. The eyes tell me more about a woman more than anything they say. You can tell so much just by studying a man or woman's eyes. I can usually tell a woman's degree of kinkiness and overall sensuality by the manner in which she uses her eyes.

I know there are some skeptics who will say, *"I don't believe you can tell all of that about a person just by their eyes."* Well, believe what you want to believe. The reality is sexually inexperienced women and/or very prudish women use their eyes far differently than women who are sexually experienced, erotically uninhibited, and/or promiscuous.

I gain enjoyment out of examining a woman's eyes, and quickly determining whether or not she is a virgin, a conservative prude, or a kinky freak.

The second physical characteristic I examine is a woman's **voice**. Women who are very kinky and promiscuous converse with men in a different manner than women who are generally conservative and prudish towards sex. Their vocal intonations are totally different.

Trust me on this: If you are a man, and you are as perceptive as me, you can learn a lot about a woman by the combination of her eyes and her voice. Most men pay attention to characteristics such as the type of clothes a woman adorns herself with.

Clothes can be misleading. A woman can be semi-prudish and be wearing a short, tight skirt. A woman can be a kinky freak and be wearing conservative clothing. I don't study men as much as women, but I would assume for very perceptive women, the same is probably true for men as well.

I said all of that to say this: I may sometimes give off the misleading impression that I am somewhat naïve and slow, but on the real, I am extremely perceptive and observant. That's not braggin, that's just keepin it real. If you are a woman or man who is generally full of shit, I will know this in the first five-to-ten minutes of our interaction, if not less. This is what gives me the credibility to write this book.

Make no mistake, no man ... including Yours Truly ... will ever understand all of the complexities of women's behavior, just like no one woman will ever understand the various aspects of men's behavior that many women find puzzling or frustrating.

I don't think figuring out all of the aspects of the opposite sex will ever be easy, and therefore, having successful and satisfying dating relationships will always be challenging to one degree or the other, but what I attempt to help men and women out with in the contents of this book is specifically related to the category of manipulative head games. I want to help men and women quickly identify manipulation.

If you cannot identify and prevent manipulative head games entirely after reading this book, at minimum, you will have a better sense of when head games are being employed with you at any given point in time, and how you can diminish the frustrating effects of them.

The fact that many men and women find dating so complicated and frustrating is exactly why the dating and relationships genre of authors, experts and gurus has exploded. Beginning with the mid-to-late 90s, and then even more so after the release of the box-office hit movie *Hitch* (starring Will Smith and Eva Mendes), you can now find Dating Coaches, Relationship Advisors, Seduction Gurus and every other variation of those three all over world in numbers.

One problem I have with many of these so-called "Seduction Community" gurus and pick-up artist mentors and advisors is that they not only fail to teach men how to recognize manipulative head games, but even worse, they teach men how to employ manipulative head games with women. I am not down with that at all.

Recently, the Attraction and Seduction Community has split off into two major factions and/or guiding philosophies:

- The Pickup Artists / Those who espouse "indirect" methods of approaching, attracting and seducing women; If you read Neil Strauss' best-selling book, *The Game: Penetrating the Secret Society of Pickup Artists*, then you know what I'm referring to. These guys are all about "pickup lines," scripts, routines, methods, and psychological and/or hypnotic techniques designed to attract and seduce women

• The Natural Conversationalists / Those who espouse being "direct" and straightforward with women regarding their romantic and/or sexual desires, interests, and intentions. I would put myself in this category, along with a few other advisors and "gurus." Authors in this category don't believe in any sort of manipulative tactics or head games.

There is nothing dumber than trying to have sex with women by pretending like you are not trying to have sex with them. The sad reality is that this is what many men in society do on a weekly basis.

The second problem I have with the "indirect" gurus is that they cause men to become afraid of rejection and harsh criticism. I don't perceive either of those reactions as "negative" or representative of "failure." I think rejection is inevitable and that negative reactions are to be expected by manipulative women.

These indirect guys contribute to the head games being played instead of making efforts to help men identify them, prevent them and diminish the use of them.

Questions:

1) How did the relationship between your mother and father affect your upbringing? Were your mother and father married, or involved in a monogamous relationship, at the time you were conceived?

2) Beginning with approximately the age of twelve or thirteen up until now, what were your general attitudes ... both positive and negative ... towards the opposite sex? Did you grow up thinking all men were lying womanizers? Did you grow up thinking that all women were manipulative, promiscuous whores?

3) What is your attitude regarding sex before marriage? Do you believe sex is something that should only be experienced between two people in a monogamous relationship? Or do you think you should be able to exchange orgasms with whomever you find sexually appealing?

4) When you converse with people, do you look them directly in their eyes? Or do you tend to look up at the ceiling, to the

right or to the left, or down at the floor? Do you study men and women's body language and behavioral tendencies?

Chapter THREE

Manipulative Head Games

There is an adage that suggests that *"You can't bullshit a bullshitter."*
I hate to tell you this, but that adage is extremely invalid. Actually,
the EASIEST person to mislead and manipulate is someone who is
trying their best to mislead and manipulate you.

Why is that? Because if I am attempting to mislead and manipulate
you, I am too busy concentrating on my own manipulative tactics to
really bother myself with identifying what manipulative tactics you
have in play. The only time a manipulator will be able to quickly
identify if you're also trying to manipulate them is if your
manipulation skills are very basic, very obvious/not subtle, and
generally weak and ineffective.

If you put two highly skilled manipulators into play with each other
… let's say one male and one female … they won't be able to quickly
identify the other person's manipulative tactics. Again, because they
will be too busy concentrating on their own manipulative tactics.

The adage **should read**, *"You can't bullshit a
STRAIGHTSHOOTER."* In my opinion, that is a more valid

statement. It is very hard to mislead, manipulate, or generally bullshit someone who is very upfront, specific, and straightforward with their desires, interests, and intentions.

Don't believe me? Let's use purchasing a car as an example:

On one end, we have "Henry." Henry is a highly manipulative used car salesman. On the other end, we have "Lisa" who is a highly manipulative car buyer.

What is Henry's objective? To sell a car that is for all practical purposes worth about $3,500.00 to Lisa for about $6,000.00

What is Lisa's objective? To buy a car that has a selling price of $6,000.00 for no more than $4,000.00

What is Henry's first move? Why of course, to play up how great that $6,000.00 automobile is.

What is Lisa's first move? To attempt to identify any obvious flaws and/or repairs that same $6,000.00 automobile is in need of.

From this point, it becomes a game of chess. Who knows more about negotiation ... Henry or Lisa? Who knows more about the true market value of a used automobile ... Henry or Lisa? Is Henry willing to sacrifice a high commission? Is Lisa willing to stretch her budget and pay more? Let the games begin.

Now, let's convert Lisa into a person who is upfront, straightforward, knows her monetary limits, and thoroughly knows the market value of used cars.

She approaches Henry and says, "That car ... I want that car for $3,750.00 ... no ifs, ands or buts." Henry says, "Are you crazy? That car is worth $6,500.00!! No less than $6,000.00!!!" Lisa says, "I'm paying no more than $3,750.00" Henry says, "Okay, okay. I'll lower it down to $5,500.00 ... how's that?" Lisa maintains. "$3,750.00"

Henry doesn't budge. Lisa begins to walk towards her current car ... then suddenly, Henry stops her. "Okay, okay. $4,000.00 That is my final offer. Lisa smirks, and says, "Okay. You have a deal."

Who won that battle? Lisa. Why? Because she was firm. She came to this used car lot knowing that she wasn't going to pay more than $4,000.00 for the automobile that Henry was trying to sell for $6,000.00. Henry could not manipulate Lisa because she was firm and specific about what she wanted.

Not feelin' that analogy? Then let's use a more dating-related one.

Henry asks Lisa out on a date. Henry really just wants a few days or a few weeks of casual sex, but he feels as though if he makes that known upfront, his desires, interests and intentions won't be enthusiastically reciprocated, so he decides to play the game of "I'm just a well-mannered gentleman looking to get to know you."

Lisa has no real romantic and/or sexual attraction to Henry, but she is never one to turn down a free lunch, a free dinner, a free movie, or a free concert. So she too decides to play the game of "I'm going to make your dumb ass THINK you might get some pussy from me in the near future, but in reality, you'll never get between my legs."

Who will win this manipulative battle? Depends. If Henry is really, really horny and desperate for sexual companionship, Lisa wins this battle EASY. Sure, as a guy, you know a lot of "Lisa" types. And surely, if you are a woman, you know a lot of "Henry" types.

The only way Henry is winning this battle is if he takes Lisa out … manages to get her sloppy drunk … and takes advantage of her … or … Henry is so loaded with cash and a willingness to offer financial favors, that Lisa looks at giving Henry some pussy as more or less an "investment" in a long-term relationship of exploiting his horny ass.

Surely, you have observed this scenario play out a hundred or more times, right? If you said, "No … this is new to me," then you are either young, naïve, or you've lived a sheltered life.

As I mentioned in Chapter Two, the two factors that have most changed dating rituals between men and women over the last forty, fifty or sixty-plus years are these:

- The increase in men and women engaging in sexual relations before marriage and/or outside the context of an exclusively committed relationship;

- The strong desire of women to use the appeal of their romantic and/or sexual companionship as a means of motivating men to spend money on them and offer them other forms of financial, non-financial, tangible and intangible "favors";

The first factor has led to manipulative head games because now you have a lot of women who practice sexual duplicity without thinking twice about it. Many women want to be the 'marrying type' and the free-spirited sex siren at once.

The second factor has led to manipulative head games because now you have many women who will "pretend" to be interested in dating a man or "pretend" to be interested in having [casual] sex with him, when in reality, they just want to be offered something of value before they tell those men that they really are not interested.

I mentioned in Chapter One that the primary criticism I have received regarding the use of Mode One Behavior is that many women (and even a few men) feel like it is "socially inappropriate" to tell a woman you have just made the acquaintance of that all you want to do is exchange orgasms with her non-monogamously for a few days, a few weeks, and/or a few months.

So ... let me get this straight: If I meet a woman who I know ahead of time that I have no interest in having a long-term, romantic, monogamous relationship with . . . but I do have an interest in having short-term, non-monogamous casual sex with . . . I should simply pretend to be a well-mannered 'gentleman,' tell this woman 'pleasant lies,' and then once I exchange orgasms with her a few times, find a way to ignore her and dump her without really hurting her feelings? Or should men avoid engaging in casual sex altogether?

Men are always going to have a desire for premarital and/or casual sex. Always. My attitude is, knowing that men desire casual sex . . .

you might as well encourage them to be straightforwardly honest about it. Then a woman can make an adult decision whether or not to reciprocate that man's desires and interests, or decline the invitation.

This is the problem with society: There are too many women (and even men too) who want to listen to pleasant lies rather than raw, real truth. And men and women wonder why so many members of the opposite sex engage in manipulative head games with one another. Men and women are always going to tell you pleasant lies if they feel there are undesirable consequences attached to telling the truth.

The end result is the brash, bold truth-tellers are being branded as the 'bad guys' in the dating and relationships arena while the smooth-talking liars and skilled manipulators are being perceived as 'well-mannered,' 'respectful,' and tactful. Yeah . . . RIGHT.

There is no in-between. Either you want lies . . . or you want truth from people. It's really that simple. *"Is lying the same thing as manipulation?"* In some respects ... yes ... and in other respects, no. Lies are a tool used to manipulate people, but I wouldn't say lying and manipulation are directly synonymous.

If I ask someone, "Are you a doctor?," and they respond *"Yes, I am a doctor,"* but then later on, I find out that this person never attended medical school at all, then this would represent a blatant liar.

A manipulator would be someone who, if asked that same question, would say, *"I know health care like the back of my hand,"* which gives you the *misleading impression* that he/she is saying, "Yes, I am a Doctor," but when you investigate, you find out that this person is a Pharmaceuticals salesperson. This person didn't flat-out lie to you, but they did not accurately tell you the truth either.

This is what manipulators do. Most manipulators don't really just flat-out lie to you. Instead, they simply mislead you into believing that they are headed in one direction, when they are actually headed in another direction.

Have you ever heard of a game used by most street con artists known as "the shell game?" I got taken once on the Chicago L(oop) train back when I was in my early twenties. The shell game involves a man or woman placing a small round ball underneath three walnut shells (or bottle caps or something similar). Then the person asks the audience who wants to bed money on where the ball is.

The trick: The person doing the shuffling gives you the misleading impression that they are the only ones involved with this game. In reality, they have about five or six people working with them.

One of the persons working with this person will pretend like he is just a regular audience member, and the person executing the shell game will pretend as though he/she doesn't initially know what they're doing. This is how they had me duped. The guy was messing up big time, and two people took his money.

I, being greedy for money, thought to myself, "This guy is trying to con people, but he doesn't know what he's doing! I will take his money!" Without getting into a long story, I lost $20.00 I was PISSED OFF. Two other people lost as much as $150.00 - $300.00

These con artists didn't exactly "lie" to their audience members, but they definitely **mislead** them. Many men make the same mistake with women that I did with these con artists. They make the mistake of thinking that their manipulative tactics will cause them to 'get over' on women, when in reality, the women are 'getting over' on the men. I see this scenario happen all of the time.

Side Note: Watch the movie Dirty Rotten Scoundrels, and Glenne Headly's character of "Janet Colgate" in particular. Janet plays the two male con artists by making them believe they are playing her. This is why I say the adage *"You can't bullshit a bullshitter"* is invalid. Janet was a master manipulator who conned two master manipulators.

Here are some of the primary motivations behind men and women engaging in manipulative head games with one another. Men pretty much only manipulate women for sex. More specifically, non-monogamous sex. Women manipulate men for money, employment opportunities, flattering attention, entertaining companionship, etc.

Why single women will attempt to manipulate men:

Motivation #1: Monetary and financial favors.

Some women will straightforwardly tell you that they want to get paid for their romantic and/or sexual companionship. These are the non-manipulative gold diggers. Street prostitutes, call girls, erotic escorts and other "ladies of the night" fall into this category.

These women are woman enough to say, "if you want to get between my legs, you will have to pay for the opportunity to do so."

Realistically, there are some women who do not want to present themselves as a street whore, a call girl, and/or an erotic escort. So, the next best thing for them to do is to engage a man in manipulative head games.

In other words, women in the latter group want to get money out of you by *pretending* that this is **not** what they're trying to do.

Women in the latter group want the perks of selling their sexual companionship without the questionable reputation that comes along with it. In my previous book, ***Mode One***, I referred to these women as "Erotic Hypocrites."

Erotic Hypocrites are many times mistaken for you typical "gold-digger," but these women are a lot craftier than your run-of-the-mill materialistic parasites (and a lot hornier). These women are subtle in their approach, and will catch you off guard if you're not on top of your game.

Motivation #2: To Live a Sexually Duplicitous Lifestyle

Some women will tell you straightforwardly that they enjoy casual, non-monogamous sex from time to time with two or more sex partners. I respect these women's honesty. Same with women who straightforwardly tell you that they enjoy very adventurous, erotically uninhibited, kinky sex (for example, occasional threesomes, sex in public, etc).

They are woman enough to say, "I'm going to enjoy my sex life in the manner that I choose to." Bravo. No haterade from me.

Realistically though, there are some women who feel as though if they were to straightforwardly admit their love for kinky sex and/or non-monogamous sex with multiple partners, they will lose their "good girl" image and reputation, and consequently, have a tougher time finding a steady boyfriend or a man willing to marry them.

So, the alternative plan is to live a sexually duplicitous lifestyle which involves misleading men into believing that the woman is an innocent, wholesome, sexually conservative "good girl" and hide their true sexuality from the 'marrying types.' In my previous book, *Mode One*, I referred to these women as "Wholesome Pretenders."

Motivation #3: To maintain a stable of men in a woman's social circle who will listen to the woman vent and keep her entertained when she is bored and/or lonely

38

Some women will tell you straightforwardly that they have no interest in dating you and that they have no interest in having [casual] sex with you. They will tell you upfront that the best you can hope for from them is a non-physical, non-sexual platonic friendship.

The vast majority of men will either choose to leave these women alone completely, or they will indefinitely suppress their romantic and/or sexual desires in order to maintain the friendship.

Realistically though, there are some women who feel like most men will not be motivated to invest the one-on-one time that they require unless they mislead these men into believing that there is at least a small percentage chance that their so-called "platonic" male friends will have the opportunity to have monogamous or non-monogamous sex with them at some point in the future.

So the other alternative is to engage in a disingenuous "play brother / play sister" relationship which has very subtle romantic and/or sexual undertones to it. The man involved says to himself, "I don't mind being her 'play brother' for now … because I know in a matter of weeks or months, she's going to ultimately let me exchange orgasms wit her." Women in this category are generally referred to as

"Attention Whores," "Dick Teasers," or simply 'Users' and/or 'Exploiters.'

As I mentioned in Chapter Two, I have a "sixth sense" for quickly identifying Manipulative Game Player types. The only guys who would get taken advantage of by a Wholesome Pretender would be a guy who mistakenly believes he's dating a woman who is monogamous-minded, when in actuality, she's being sexed up by three or four different guys. I have probably taken advantage of Wholesome Pretenders far, far more than vice versa.

I had a woman at one of my book signing events in 2007 admit to me that she fell into the third category of female manipulators (i.e., Attention Whores, Dick Teasers, etc). She said, "Alan ... I'm going to be honest. I never tell my male [platonic] friends straightforwardly that they will never, ever get the opportunity to date me or have sex with me. Never. If I did that, probably 90% of my male friends would stop calling me and stop hanging out with me socially. So, I would never be stupid enough to destroy their hopes."

In other words, she was bluntly admitting to me that she loves to mislead and manipulate men. Of course, when I put it in those words, she was reluctant to categorize her behavior as "manipulative." She chose to call it "smart and advantageous behavior for a woman." She says tomayto, I say tomahto. Men, make no mistake: If you allow yourself to engage in those unproductive "Play Brother / Play Sister" type friendships with women, you are essentially inviting a woman to **manipulate** you.

I had another woman say to me at a book signing event in California, "Alan, I thought you knew … ALL women … to one degree or another … are manipulative. I don't know too many non-manipulative women." And again, this came from a woman's mouth.

Do women engage in more manipulative head games than men? Or in your experience, do men engage in more head games than women?

I would say both genders are guilty.

In my observation, women engage in more manipulative head games because of a higher number of different motivations than the average manipulative man. I've known women to use their "feminine charms" and sex appeal to manipulate male police officers into not writing them a speeding ticket.

Men are easy targets for manipulation by women because the average man is two-to-three times more horny for quick, casual non-monogamous "let's fuck right now" type sex than the average woman is. Within the context of a long-term monogamous relationship, I find women to be just as horny, if not hornier for sex than most men are, but when you are talking meet someone at 8:00pm and wanting to exchange orgasms with them by 8:15pm, men are the horniest.

Now for the women reading this book, let's highlight some motivations behind men's manipulative ways.

Why single men will attempt to manipulate women:

Motivation #1:   To Get Women Who Don't Normally Engage in Short-Term Sex to Engage in Short-Term Sex

Some men will tell women straightforwardly that they just want to engage in a brief, torrid love affair that will soon end with fond memories for both parties involved. I respect that. That is part of the essence of what Mode One Behavior is all about.

These men are willing to put their "well-mannered gentleman" reputations on the line, and run the risk of being described as a "heart breaker" or "ladies' man." They realize that these are nothing more than subjective labels anyhow.

Realistically, there are a number of men in society who are "wolves in sheep's clothing." They will give a woman the misleading impression that they are only in the market for a long-term "serious girlfriend," but in reality, they only want to engage in a few weeks or months of hot, kinky sex with the type of woman who most men would want as a steady girlfriend. They will usually date each woman for anywhere from six weeks to five or six months.

Men in the latter group want to enjoy the sexual pleasures of a full-blown player or womanizer, but they don't want their true desires and intentions to be advertised on their foreheads. They feel they might 'scare' some potential sex partners away, particularly those who are classy-looking and very attractive. So they pretend to play the "monogamous-minded gentleman" role with women, but in reality, they are on the hunt for new and different short-term sex partners.

The key thing with these guys is, these men don't want to have casual sex with women who regularly or normally have short-term sexual relationships. They want to have short-term monogamous sex with women who have a history of only engaging in **long-term** monogamous sexual relationships.

These men are often referred to as "Playboys" (not to be confused with 'players') and/or "Serial Monogamists."

Motivation #2: To Live a Sexually Duplicitous Lifestyle

There are some men who are true, straight-up 'players.' They will have three or four different sex partners, and each of the man's sex partners know that they are having sex with other women.

I totally respect that. You tell your group of sex partners what the program is, and they are either down with the program or not.

Realistically, some men don't have the cojones to tell a woman candidly and straightforwardly that they want to have sex with her and a number of other women. These men are too afraid of having a woman reject the idea of sharing a man with other women sexually.

Therefore, these men plain and simply lie to women. For example, a man in this category will have three different sex partners, but each of those three women will be under the misguided belief that she is that man's "exclusively committed sex partner." These poor, naïve women.

These men sometimes fancy themselves as "players," but in reality, they are not. Not even close. These men are usually referred to as "Dogs" and/or "Lying womanizers."

<u>Motivation #3</u>: To Get Women to Have Sex with Them by Pretending as though Sex is the Last Thing On Their Mind

Most men realize that their underlying reason for wanting to date any woman is sex. Whether they want a long-term relationship or short-term relationship or a monogamous relationship or a non-monogamous relationship, these men realize that ultimately, dating comes down to the desire to exchange pleasurable orgasms with a woman.

Some men let this desire be known upfront and straightforwardly. They make it clear that they are not looking for anything platonic in any way, shape, or form with any single, unattached woman. You have to respect a man who is not afraid to let his manly desires be known from the get-go.

Realistically though, there are some men who believe that the most effective means of getting a woman to have sex with them is to hide, deny, and/or camouflage their sexual desires. These men basically behave indefinitely as though sex is the absolute last thing on their mind.

Men in this category will do things like spend a lot of time engaging in entertaining small talk with women, making them laugh, performing both financial and non-financial favors for them, and generally treating women like "play sisters" and princesses.

These men foolishly believe that these women will one day show their gratitude for all of the favors executed by becoming their girlfriend, "friend-with-benefits," or short-term sex partner. In my previous book, *Mode One*, I referred to these men as "Mode Three Targets." Some people refer to these men as "weasels."

The feigned "play brother / play sister" relationship is what I refer to as **FunClubbing**. I've discussed this on my talk radio show as well as many blogs, message boards, discussion forums, and in many of my television and radio interviews.

Most men are dreadfully afraid to express their desire for non-monogamous sex to women in an upfront, straightforward manner. Again, this is over half of the reason I wrote *Mode One*. Women know that the average man is scared to straightforwardly ask for a one-night stand, a weekend fling, a friends-with-benefits situation, and they take advantage of it.

If you read *Mode One: Let the Women Know What You're REALLY Thinking*, you already know how I feel about being afraid to express your true desires, interests and intentions to women.

If you don't remember anything else after reading this book, it is imperative that you have the concept below memorized:

MANIPULATION IS ALWAYS A TWO-WAY STREET.

Adult men and women who employ manipulative tactics themselves are usually the primary people who become victims of manipulation. This is what I already pointed out at the beginning of the chapter: It is much easier for someone to 'get over on you' when you're trying to 'get over on them.' The only reason you got duped was because you were trying to dupe someone yourself.

So before you go pointing the finger at that man or woman for being "oh-so-manipulative," take a look in the mirror first. What are you up to? Are you a straightshooter or a misleading manipulator? Be real. Straightshooters only experience one of two responses from others: reciprocation and/or rejection. There really is no in-between.

If I approach a woman at a social gathering, and I say, "I want to have casual sex with you for the next four-to-six weeks … nothing monogamous, no wining and dining, no holding hands in the park on a Saturday afternoon … just good, enjoyable episodes of exchanging orgasms," what can that woman really do, other than reciprocate my interests or reject my interests? Very little, if anything.

I'm going to get into more full detail about manipulative men and women in subsequent chapters, but here is an early clue to the primary characteristic of manipulative people ... particularly as it relates to dating and relationships:

MANIPULATIVE PEOPLE DON'T LIKE TO BE PUT IN A POSITION WHERE THEY HAVE TO BE UPFRONT AND STRAIGHTFORWARD REGARDING WHAT THEY WANT FROM YOU or DON'T WANT FROM YOU.

Remember that. Mark it down. Keep that in your mind indefinitely. The quickest way to frustrate a manipulative man or woman is to put them in a position where they have to be upfront and straightforward in terms of communicating to you what they want from you or don't want from you. This interferes with the games they desire to play.

Manipulative people don't like to give you a quick, definite "yes" or a quick, definite "no." Manipulative people like to be vague and ambiguous when it comes to expressing their romantic and/or sexual desires, interests and intentions. They like to "beat-around-the-bush."

Manipulative people like to say things like "We'll see…" or "maybe, maybe not," or "kinda, sorta." Vague bullshit statements like that. They don't like specificity. They like room to "fudge" and toy with people. Manipulative people love to be flakey and wishy-washy.

Manipulative people don't like to say, "Yes, I will …." or "No, I won't …" Manipulative people like to "keep you guessing." Have you ever had a conversation with someone, and at the conclusion of the conversation, you could not really remember half of what they talked about? You felt confused … puzzled? That's because you just got finish talking to a person who is generally full of shit. A disingenuous manipulator. That's what they do. They talk a lot, but they don't really say anything that is specific or definite.

Straightshooters use very few words to get their point across. They say what they mean, and mean what they say. Everything is to-the-point, firm, upfront, specific, and candid. They tell you what they want, and how much time, money, and/or effort they are willing to give up to get what they want. They don't fudge. They don't use vague, ambiguous, and/or convoluted language.

You guessed it ... more questions:

1) When was the last time you felt 'used,' exploited, or manipulated? Were you left feeling angry, frustrated, resentful and/or bitter?

2) If you are a man, have you ever pretended to be interested in a long-term, monogamous relationship when you knew you just wanted casual sex? Have you ever pretended to be content with a platonic friendship when you knew deep-down that you wanted to date that woman or have casual sex with that woman? Why did you do that?

3) If you are a woman, have you ever continued to remain "just friends" with a man despite the fact that you knew he wanted to date you or have casual sex with you? Why? How important is flattering attention from men to you? How important is financial favors from men to you? How important is it to have a man entertain you (in a non-sexual manner) when you are bored and lonely?

Chapter FOUR

Mode One Behavior
and
Manipulative Game Players

Based on all of my adult years interacting with the opposite gender, I have come to the conclusion that every person you are interested in dating or having sex with will generally fall into two categories, and then even more specifically, two sub-categories within each of the main two categories.

The starting point of identifying what man or woman falls into what category depends specifically on what are your interests? What are your romantic and/or sexual desires, interests, and intentions with the person you are interacting with at the moment?

You will never be able to accurately identify the type of people you are dealing with if you don't know your own motivations for interacting with this person. Personally, I believe at any given moment in time **you always know** why you are interacting with a member of the opposite sex.

Revisit those six types of relationships I discussed in Chapter Two (e.g., long-term monogamous, long-term non-monogamous, et al). You might try to fool others ... and even to an extent, yourself, but deep-down, you ALWAYS know what you want from a member of the opposite sex. Usually, it is going to be physical intimacy, emotional attachment, loyal support, respect, money and/or financial favors and employment favors, to be entertained when you are bored, to be flattered when your ego and self-esteem need a boost, or some other tangible and/or intangible benefit your mind leads you to believe is desirable to you.

Once you have good idea of what your own romantic and/or sexual desires, interests and intentions are, then you can begin to develop a knack for evaluating what men or women are manipulative or non-manipulative, and share the same interests as you or do not share the same interests as you.

Mode Two Behavior will not help you identify Manipulative Game Players. Mode Two Behavior is too cautious and involves too much vague and ambiguous type conversation. Mode Three Behavior will not help you identify Manipulative Game Players. You are too busy hiding, denying and camouflaging your own desires and interests to recognize the true desires and interests of others.

Only Mode One Behavior truly helps you identify manipulative types from non-manipulative types. When you are Mode One, here are the four general types of women (and men) you will run into:

Straightshooters	Reciprocators
	Rejecters
Manipulative Game Players	Pretenders
	Timewasters

There really are no other categories that those you interact with will fall into. Any man or woman you choose to interact with at any given moment in time is going to be a Reciprocator, a Rejecter, a Pretender, or a Timewaster.

As you can predict, Straightshooters are far easier to deal with in the long-run than Manipulative Game Players. Straightshooters say what they mean, and mean what they say. The whole purpose of this book is really designed to teach you how to identify and deal with Pretenders and Timewasters.

Since I'm attempting to make this book somewhat "balanced" between advice to men and advice for women (even though in reality, it is not my specialty to be giving advice to women on dating and relationships ... I'm all about helping out the *"frustrated nice guys"* out in the world), how I define each member of each category will be different depending on gender.

For example, a "male timewaster" is different than a "female timewaster." There really are not any "male Pretenders." That category is almost exclusively female. If a man has the same romantic and/or sexual interests as a woman, he is going to let her know his interests in an upfront and straightforward manner.

Timewasters are different. For example, many men would consider a woman a "timewaster" if she's not offering him the opportunity to have sex with her. Many women would call a man a timewaster if he's only looking for sex. **Different gender, different perspective**.

So again, I'm going to try to give both genders advice on manipulative head games, but there will more-than-likely be at least a slight lean towards helping single men identify manipulative women more so than helping out single women identify manipulative men.

Question to women:

When a man expresses his romantic and/or sexual desires, interests and intentions to you in an upfront, straightforward manner ... what prevents you from either straightforwardly reciprocating his desires or straightforwardly rejecting his desires and interests?

Question to men:

Are you able to very quickly and effectively identify a manipulative woman from a non-manipulative woman?

Chapter FIVE

Reciprocators

Of the four categories of men and women you will interact with, none will be more enjoyable and easy to deal with than those men and women who are totally willing to reciprocate your romantic and/or sexual desires, interests and intentions.

I don't really need to offer you any words of wisdom regarding a Reciprocator. The only thing I would emphasize when dealing with men and women in this group is that it is imperative that you let the men and women in your life know exactly what you are looking for, and exactly why you want to share their company (in other words, exhibit Mode One Behavior).

If you fail to do this, you end up confusing a "Reciprocator" with a "Timewaster," which I will talk about in more detail in Chapter Eight.

At the risk of generalizing by gender, I will say that based on my experiences and observations, men are far more likely to reciprocate a woman's desires and interests straightforwardly much more than the average woman will … particularly as it relates to [casual] sex.

Men are not known for making women "jump through hoops" in order to engage in casual sex. Women do that quite frequently.

In an ideal world, all men and women should find no reason not to reciprocate each other's romantic and/or sexual desires, interests and intentions if they both share the same desires and interests.

In my lifetime, no more than 10-15% of the women I've met have been reciprocators. I love these women. These women are not looking for any incentives or rewards in exchange for their monogamous or non-monogamous sexual companionship. These women are not looking to engage in any sort of 'ego battles' or head games. These women are genuine, down-to-earth, and non-manipulative.

If a woman is a Reciprocator, then once you tell her that you have some desires and interests that are in line with her own, she's like, "let's go for it." Trust me fellas ... when you meet a woman like this, treasure it. These women are the diamond in the haystack.

The only 'catch' with Reciprocators is that sometimes you might confuse a Reciprocator with a Timewaster. Again, this is over half of the reason why I wrote this book. To help men (and women) distinguish between Straightshooters and Manipulative Game Players, to distinguish Reciprocators from Timewasters, and to distinguish Rejecters from Pretenders.

The only behavior that will allow you to do that is **Mode One Behavior**. When you exhibit Mode Two Behavior (i.e., expressing your desires and interests in a manner which is vague, ambiguous, overly cautious, indecisive, etc.) or Mode Three Behavior (i.e., hiding your true desires and interests, denying your interests, camouflaging your interests, etc.) you will never be able to distinguish what woman falls into what category.

Let's be clear on what reciprocation is: If a man or woman adds some sort of "condition" or incentive or reward, then that is not reciprocation. That is manipulation. If a woman says, "Alan, can I borrow $500.00 until two weeks from now?" and I say, "Sure. No problem." That is reciprocation.

If that woman asks me that same favor, and I say, "Well … if you give me five blowjobs over the next two weeks, then yeah … I'll go ahead and loan you the money …" then that is not reciprocation. That is manipulation.

Common question from men who read **_Mode One_**:

"So wait a minute Alan. Are you saying that if I have an interest in simply a one night erotic tryst with a woman, I should just approach her, and tell her what I'm REALLY THINKING? Won't I get slapped or cursed out?"

A non-manipulative straightshooter would never have an adverse reaction to upfront, straightforward honesty. Never. A Pretender and/or Timewaster might. Not a Reciprocator. Women who are Reciprocators welcome bold, straightforward honesty (this is not simply my opinion … women tell me this literally on a monthly, if not weekly basis).

Cherish every moment you are able to enjoy interacting with a Reciprocator. This is the group where your "soulmates" will usually come from.

Question to men:

When you express your romantic and/or sexual desires, interests and intentions to women in a Mode One manner, how do they generally respond to you?

Question to women:

What is your greatest fear of straightforwardly reciprocating a man's desires and interests, assuming your desires and interests are the same as his?

Chapter SIX

Rejecters

Be honest: Are you afraid of rejection? Answer that question for yourself. In the meantime, pretend that I have met this fictitious woman named "Brenda."

Brenda is so fine. She is one super sexy woman. Nice breasts. Nice butt. Intelligent. Articulate. Well-read. I want to date this woman very, very badly. I think about Brenda every day of the week.

I approach Brenda, let her know that I'm attracted to her . . . only for her to say, *"Alan, you are so not my type. We can be platonic friends though!!"* Forget that "platonic friends" crap. I don't want to be any woman's "play brother."

As a man, have you felt this way after receiving a similar response? You have your eyes set on one attractive, quality woman … and she breaks your heart and/or crushes your ego by telling you that you are "not her type." Ain't that a bitch.

When I was younger, I sometimes had a tough time handling rejection. I would assume all men who are roughly thirty-five years of age or younger have had a tough time dealing with being rejected.

You think it is an indictment on what you have or don't have to offer. Sometimes, when you are rejected by a woman ... you think this means that you are not attractive enough, not sexy enough, not wealthy enough, not intelligent enough and not entertaining enough to maintain this woman's interest. Poor you.

Back to this woman named Brenda. Fast forward to one year later where I'm hangin with my boys, and one of them says, *"Yo Al . . . you remember that chick Brenda you used to be crazy about?"* Of course, I'm like, "why do you have to bring HER up?!?"

My friend: *"Man ... the dude she started dating after you met her is in jail."* Jail? Huh? *"Evidently, he found out she was pregnant with his best friend's baby and on top of that, she left some cocaine in homeboy's car which caused him to get cited for possession. He lost his temper and beat her ass. Now, ol' dude is locked up."*

Well, well, well. Isn't Ms. Brenda a piece of work. Fine, sexy Brenda. The woman who I once thought might be "the one."

How would I feel? Why of course I would feel vindicated. Of course I would feel like, 'whew … glad that wasn't me who got caught up." I know some of you reading my book might be atheist or agnostic, but my belief is, Rejection is God's Protection.

The MAN UPSTAIRS knows who you need to be with and who you don't need to be with. HE usually gives you signs. HE will provide you with certain "red flags" … either overt or subtle. You can choose to pay attention or not.

I have reached a point in my life where I no longer fear rejection from a woman. My attitude is, "if it's meant for me to interact with a woman, date a woman, and enjoy pleasurable orgasms with a woman, an opportunity will be provided to me."

I have found myself many times saying to myself, "In retrospect, I am so glad I never dater HER." It is similar to having your shuttle bus get you to the airport late, and you miss your flight … and you are angry, using profanity and throwing a hissy fit … until … you find out that the plane you missed had electrical trouble and crashed.

You are now like, "Wow. Thank GOD I wasn't on that plane." Changes your perspective on not getting your way, doesn't it?

Trust me on this: **Rejection is always WIN / WIN.**

If a woman is genuinely just not interested in you, and has no real romantic or sexual attraction to you, then her rejecting you is saving you TIME and MONEY. When you are young, you don't realize that as much as you do when you reach the age of thirty-five and older. TIME IS PRECIOUS. Don't waste time pursuing women who have no interest in you. I will talk about this in a little more detail in Chapter Eight.

You didn't waste time ... You didn't waste money ... WIN.

If a woman rejects you, but deep-down, she really is attracted to you physically, romantically and sexually ... then she is a Pretender (who I will discuss in the next chapter). And 90% chance or more, this woman is going to make an effort to communicate with you again sometime in the future. And just who will have the "upper hand" in this relationship now? YOU will.

She rejected me initially ... but she got in contact with me later on ... Another WIN for you

Rejection is more painful and frustrating when it comes <u>after</u> you have invested a high amount of time and/or money.

Many dating and relationships advisors, authors, and gurus make thousands and thousands of dollars leading you to believe that the absolute worst thing that could ever happen to you in the world of dating is to get rejected by a woman. And you know what? That is some BULLSIIIT.

How would you ever hook up with the RIGHT person if none of the WRONG [potential] companions ever rejected you? Rejection is a natural part of the rituals of dating. Not every woman you meet is going to have the same desires as you or the same interests as you. Some women will find you too short, too fat, too poor, not ambitious enough, not funny enough, etc. SO? Why would you want to be with a woman who treats a $1,000,000.00 cashier's check (you) like a $10.00 money order (their perception of you)?

You cannot succeed with women if you are profoundly afraid of rejection. That would be like a top-notch home run hitting baseball player being dreadfully afraid of striking out. Striking out happens to all home run champions. Do you think Barry Bonds walked up to the plate afraid of striking out? Babe Ruth? Hank Aaron? C'mon fellas. Puhleaze.

Don't read or purchase any dating advice book that makes you feel like if you get rejected, you are doing something "wrong" ... or failing to do something "right." In a few cases ... yeah, well maybe. But in most cases? The woman is simply NOT INTERESTED. It was not meant to be. Move on to the next woman.

WIN / WIN Baby.

Same goes for women. If a man loses interest in you because you told him you choose to wait until you are married before having sex, then that is his loss. Do not have sex with a man because he pressures you to, or makes you feel obligated to do so.

I say you should appreciate each and every man or woman in your life who rejects you in an upfront, straightforward manner. You will be over that rejection in a matter of minutes, hours, or a few days. If you asked me to write a list of the last twenty-five women who rejected me and my interests, I wouldn't be able to do it.

But I guarantee you . . . if you asked me to write down a list of the last ten-to-fifteen women who caused me to waste time and/or money, I could write down their first name, last name, middle name, their grandmother's name ... and so on. Okay, I lied about the last two. But you get my point.

You want to look out for Timewasters more than Rejecters. Rejecters are not the "bad guys" (or "gals"). Not at all. They are helping you move one step closer to the men and women you are supposed to be interacting with.

Men, if a woman states her lack of interest in you in a firm, crystal clear, straightforward manner ... please ... leave her alone. I receive a number of comments and complaints from women telling me how many men just can't handle or accept rejection. I'm not talking about women who express the "slow no" variation. I'm talking about women who look you dead in your eyes and say to you, "I have no interest in sharing your company in a romantic or sexual manner."

Leave her alone.

The fear of rejection is what causes men to exhibit Mode Three Behavior just like the fear of harsh criticism causes men to exhibit Mode Two Behavior. Do not fall into that trap. Express your desires and interests to women in an upfront, straightforwardly honest manner and leave the rest up to them.

The fear of rejection comes from "attaching" yourself to a specific and/or expected result, reaction or response. Do not allow your ego to become attached to a specific result. The result is ultimately out of your hands.

Never allow yourself to be in a position where you feel as though you "need" a man or woman's romantic and/or sexual companionship. Only allow yourself to **want** their companionship. When you allow yourself to need men or women's companionship, you open the door for them to treat you in an undesirable and/or disrespectful manner.

Accept rejection quickly and gracefully.

Questions:

1) When a man or woman fails to reciprocate your romantic and/or sexual interests (i.e., they reject you), do you generally take a long time to get over being rejected?

2) Think about the last time a man or woman expressed an interest in dating you and/or having sex with you. Did you let that person know in an upfront and straightforward manner that you were not interested? Or did you go the coward's route and simply 'blow them off' (e.g., fail to return their phone calls, ignored their Email messages, etc.)

3) Have you ever pretended to be interested in someone for a short period of time simply because you didn't have the courage to reject that person?

4) Think of a time when a man or woman rejected you, but then weeks, months, or years later, you found out a number of characteristics about the person who rejected you that made you feel glad that you had never dated them or had sex with them. Did that make you feel better later on? Did you feel vindicated?

Chapter SEVEN

Pretenders

It's a lot of real G's doin' time
'Cuz a groupie bent the truth and told a lie.
You picked the wrong guy,
baby if you're too fly
You need to hit the door,
search for a new guy.
'Cuz I only got one night in town,
Break down or be clowned,
Baby doll are you down?
I get around

Lyrics from the late Tupac Shakur's rap song, ***I Get Around***

Now please tell me you are not naïve enough to believe that everyone who is interesting in dating you or having sex with you is just going to tell you in an upfront and straightforward manner without any drama or challenge to your ego? No way.

Similarly, tell me you are not so inexperienced to think that because a member of the opposite sex does not share the same romantic and/or sexual interests as you, that they are just going to dismiss you and quickly move on to the next person. Uhm . . . . no.

70

Women … you might as well bypass this chapter and move on to Chapter Eight. I will be with you in a moment. The reason being is, realistically, there are very few, if any men who validly fall into the category of a "Pretender."

If a woman expresses to a man that she has an interest in a long-term monogamous relationship … and a man feels the same way … 99.99% chance, he is going to reciprocate. If a woman expresses to a man that she has an interest in only casual sex … and a man feels the same way … 99.999999% chance, he is going to quickly reciprocate.

Men very rarely, if ever, "pretend" not to have the same romantic and/or sexual interests in a woman, only to acknowledge similar interests later on. Pretenders are virtually always women. Men are usually Reciprocators, Rejecters, or Timewasters.

Fellas, get ready for some real talk. Get your notepads out, and jot down some thoughts. There will be a lot of harsh, provocative, even X-rated talk in this chapter and the next, so if you consider yourself a conservative person or a deeply religious person, this content might make you blush. **You have been warned.** Read this chapter at your own risk.

If you are a father to a daughter fifteen years of age or older, there is a good chance you told your daughter to stay away from the 'loser' types. The ones who are earning bad grades, use profanity and bad grammar, get into fights all of the time, and just generally cause trouble in the neighborhood. You want your daughter with good guys with a promising future and good, wholesome intentions, right?

Please tell me that you didn't really think she was going to follow that advice did you. Shame on you. There is at least a 50% chance right now that your daughter is somewhere exchanging orgasms with that very 'loser' type who you spoke of; That 'loser' is fu**ing your daughter in the back seat of a car with a vengeance. He knows you and others perceive him as a 'loser,' so he is taking out his vindictive frustration on your daughter while his manhood is inside her vagina.

Too harsh? I'm not here to give you advice about life, dating and relationships in a "G-rated" style manner. This is real life baby.

That guy who you perceive as the 'loser' type is the proverbial "bad boy." That bad boy knows how to break your daughter down and get her panties wet. Performing such a feat is an art form for him.

"Damnit Alan! Why do you have to be so cynical and graphic!! My daughter is a 'good girl' who makes all of the right decisions!! Her

mind is not corrupted!!" Yeah, okay. You keep telling yourself that to make yourself sleep better at night. The reality is, your teenage daughter is somewhere right now on her knees giving a 'bad boy' an enthusiastic blowjob. Whatever you do, don't be a naïve parent.

Let's say you are in high school. As the "nice guy" in the neighborhood, you hear your platonic female friend "Michelle" refer to her ex-boyfriend "T-Dog" as a thug, a loser, an asshole, a liar, a dog, and every other highly subjective and insulting label in the book.

Guess what though Mr. Nice Guy? T-Dog is exchanging orgasms with Michelle anytime he wants to, and all you get to do is listen to Michelle vent about T-Dog's so-called undesirable behavior. Doesn't that frustrate you? I mean, really. T-Dog is your classic "bad boy."

Michelle tells her girlfriends that you are a good guy, a "sweetie," very intelligent, very funny, enjoyable to play pool with and go bowling with … right? Then how come you can't even get Michelle to give you a kiss? T-Dog is getting sex regularly from Michelle. Michelle is T-Dog's personal kinky freak. You are Michelle's "play brother." The guy she counts on to entertain her and comfort her.

Are you feelin' me Mr. Nice Guy? You see, you have Michelle on a pedestal . . . you already have her branded as "marriage material" …

but yet T-Dog has his way with Michelle. She is nothing but just ONE of his many kinky freaks in his cell phone contact list.

"So what you're saying Alan is … 'bad boys' get all of the women, and the 'nice guys' like me can only hope for platonic friendship at best? Wow. That's messed up." Nice guys don't get the punani. Let's start at the beginning, shall we?

If you are the teenager Michelle's mother and/or father, you took her to church every Sunday. Michelle was in Sunday School just about every week. Michelle earned a B+ or higher in all of her classes.

When you gave her the "birds and bees" talk, you let her know that her sexual companionship is best reserved for marriage, or at minimum, some guy who she is deeply in love with.

You, Mr. Nice Guy, were taught by your mother to be a "well-mannered gentleman," and to exhibit socially appropriate behavior around all of the young ladies so they will go home and tell their parents that you are a really good guy. A guy who the teenage girl's parents could trust their daughter to go out on a date with.

You know what Mr. Bad Boy said to all of those rules of etiquette? He said, "I follow my own rules." Mr. Bad Boy lives by his own guidelines for what is appropriate. He behaves in whatever manner he feels is conducive to achieving his desired objectives. You don't like Mr. Bad Boy's behavior? SO. Don't like his tattoos or earrings? SO. Don't like his profane language? SO. Don't like his seemingly lack of career ambition? SO. Like Mr. Bad Boy really cares about what YOU think of him and what YOUR opinion of him is.

You see Mr. Nice Guy, if a woman can predict your behavior too frequently, you soon become boring to her. If when she says "jump," and you respond by saying, "how high?" right there you have lost any chance of ever dating her or having sex with this woman.

A woman with an ego who has a high desire to manipulate men wants a challenge. She wants a man who is intriguing to her. A man who is going to pass all of her "tests." *"Tests? What tests??"*

Some of the tests administered by a Manipulative Game Player:

Test #1: Are you afraid of being rejected by me? Does it bother you to be indefinitely ignored by me?

Didn't we just get finished talking about rejection in the last chapter? Of course we did. Most men do everything possible to prevent themselves from being rejected and/or ignored by a woman who they find attractive and sexy. Most high school guys, college guys, and men in their twenties want to be associated with the women who are popular, attractive, and sexy. Everyone knows this.

Don't you think women know this? Oh .. you didn't know that? Shame on you bro. In **Mode One**, I talked about the negative effects of the classroom bully. The bully says, *"you better do what I say or I'm going to kick your ass."* A manipulative woman has a similar mindset. *"you better do what I say and behave in a manner that I approve of, or otherwise I'm going to act like I don't know you and indefinitely ignore you."* Do you let women 'punk' you like this?

Nice Guy types punk out. They give in. They say all of the right things in the right way without even thinking about taking a chance at pissing a woman off. No way. You play up to her ego. You offer to wine and dine her. You listen to all of her boring stories. **You are better than having a puppy.** Why wouldn't any woman say anything but great things about you? You are truly MR. NICE GUY.

The Mr. Bad Boys of society could care less if these women threaten to ignore them. They have enough women in their stable for it not to matter. Do you think a man with balls is going to attempt to say "the right thing in the right manner?" Puhleaze. Wake up.

Mr. Bad Boy is going to say whatever the hell he feels like saying. Oh, a woman doesn't like how Mr. Bad Boy expresses himself verbally? SO. The Bad Boy types are immune to games. They just don't allow themselves to get sucked into such silly behavior.

Bad Boy types don't live their life to please, impress, and/or accommodate women with spoiled egos and manipulative tendencies. They don't play that game. A Bad Boy type could care less if women choose to indefinitely ignore him. SO WHAT.

Hey Mr. Nice Guy, you not only want a woman's attention and companionship, but rather you **need** it. Your ego and your self-esteem have to have it. Consequently, you fail this test.

Test #2: Are you afraid of being harshly criticized by me? Does it bother you to have me call you derogatory names and insult you? You don't want me to label you a 'jerk' do you?

Hey Mr. Nice Guy. I know the second most significant fear you have next to the fear of being rejected and/or ignored. You are afraid of "Ms. Woman of Your Dreams" having an adverse reaction to anything you say. You would never want to be labeled an 'asshole' or a 'jerk', now would you? Of course not. Your ego is way too sensitive to harsh criticisms.

Any attractive woman can get you to shape up totally to her preferences just by threatening to call you an undesirable name. Don't you realize that anyone with a spoiled ego who doesn't get their way is going to become angry with you? That is human nature my friend. What do subjective labels mean to you anyway?

Bad Boy types don't live their life to win favorable opinions and flattering compliments from women with spoiled egos and manipulative tendencies. They don't play that game. A Bad Boy type could care less if women choose to harshly criticism him and insult him to their girlfriends behind his back. SO WHAT.

Test #3: You better offer me some sort of incentive or reward for sharing your company. If you spend money on me I might just let you masturbate on the idea and visualization of having sex with me. Did you hear that?

"No way Alan. No young lady who was raised in a Christian home thinks like this!! Aren't you going a bit overboard?? I mean, there are genuine 'good girls' you know."

You are right. There are some women who are "genuine good girls" (i.e., not manipulative, good morals and values, want to only have sex with a man who is their husband, fiancé, or long-time boyfriend, etc.).

The reality is the genuine good girls probably make up about 10-15% of the single women in society. Maybe 20-25% if I'm being generous. The vast majority of single women have had at least one Bad Boy type 'turn them out' (i.e., got the previously 'innocent' and 'wholesome' woman to unleash/reveal their hidden kinky side).

Many single women who are manipulative, calculating, spoiled, kinky and even promiscuous are **playing the role** of a "good girl." This is what I refer to as a "Wholesome Pretender" or "Erotic Hypocrite." They play the 'good girl' role as well as any fictional character that feature-film legend Meryl Streep has ever played on celluloid.

You see, once an attractive woman discovers that there are hundreds, if not thousands of super horny men out in society ready to flatter her ego at the drop of a dime, spend money on her to no ends, and pretty much do whatever she asks just for at least **one opportunity to get between her legs**, it is at the moment that a woman discovers the "power of the pussy." That 'power' is very addicting for women.

Men get new jobs to get in a woman's pants. Men purchase more expensive clothes, more expensive automobiles, and more expensive houses just to gain the opportunity to slide their erect penis in and out of the vagina of a really attractive, sexy, but seemingly inaccessible woman. Let's just keep it real: **Over half of what motivates a man to do damn near EVERYTHING he does is to ATTRACT ONE or MORE DESIRABLE SEXUAL COMPANIONS.**

A man wanting to get laid is not what opens the door for manipulative head games to take place. As I mentioned in *Mode One*, it is when you start offering women incentives and rewards in exchange for their romantic and sexual companionship that the games begin.

———

No Games:

Alan: "I want to exchange orgasms with you."
Desirable Woman: *"Okay. I'm attracted to you Alan, so I wouldn't have a problem with that."*
Alan: "Cool."

———

Head Games:

Alan: "I want to exchange orgasms with you."
Desirable Woman: *"What do I look like ... some sort of street whore? Some sort of airhead slut? You better show me some respect and come to me correct Mr. Man! Do I look like I have 'I'm an easy lay' on my forehead? You better take me to a fancy restaurant!! Men!"*

<u>What the woman is really saying with this "theatrical" reaction</u>: Alan, you need to offer me some sort of incentive or reward in exchange for me allowing you to have sex with me. I need to be flattered. I need to be wined and dined. I need to be made to feel 'special.' If you don't behave in the manner that is to my ego's liking, I'm not going to speak to you again. I'm going to dislike you, talk trash about you, and indefinitely ignore you.

Naïve Alan: "She's a Rejecter!"
Experienced Alan: "She's a Pretender."

Pretenders get mistaken for Rejecters all of the time by men who are inexperienced with women. What is the difference?

Rejecters, as explained in the previous chapter, are not interested in you. These women have no desire to date you or have sex with you whatsoever. And they are not afraid to tell you that to your face.

Pretenders on the other hand are women who potentially have some degree of attraction to you and interest in you, but **if you fail their tests**, they actually do lose interest.

You have virtually a 0% chance of getting a woman who is a Rejecter to show any interest in you. I don't care if you get a better job, lose weight, win the lottery, become rich and famous ... whatever. Women who are Rejecters will never become interested in you beyond maybe possibly a platonic friendship.

With Pretenders, it can go either way. Their interest in you can significantly **increase** or **decrease**. Revisit my opening quote from Chapter Two in my previous book, *Mode One*. The woman who was quoted in *Essence* magazine. She is a classic example of a Pretender. You've heard the term, "what separates the men from the boys." Pretenders separate the men with balls from the men without balls. Pretenders separate the 'nice guys' from the 'bad boys.' Pretenders separate the men who can be easily manipulated from those men who it is next-to-impossible to manipulate.

Have you ever had a woman give you her a phone number, but when you called her, she never returned your phone call? She might tell you she is "busy," but that is simply a manipulative "test."

She wants to see how long you can be ignored by her before it bothers you, and you begin demanding to receive attention from her. I know men who have made the mistake of calling women administering such a test two times, five times, even ten times without that woman calling them back. These guys failed her manipulative test. No sexual companionship for them. The Pretender has lost interest.

The reason why that woman is not returning your calls is because you have already proved to her that you cannot be ignored by her. That is a major turn-off to a Pretender. Pretenders want a challenge.

Fundamental rule to remember about Pretender types:

If you pass one or more of a Pretender's manipulative head games tests, nine times out of ten, their romantic and/or sexual interest in you will **increase** as the days, weeks, and months go by; If you fail one or more of a Pretender's manipulative head games tests, nine times out of ten, their interest in dating you or having sex with you is going to significantly **decrease** over time.

As a man, think of a time when you met a woman … and initially, it seemed like this woman was absolutely crazy over you. Then, as quickly as two or three weeks later, this woman behaved as though she was totally uninterested in you. I've had that happen at least nine or ten times in my adult life … particularly when I was younger.

I didn't realize it at the time, but I was dealing with a Pretender. Now that I'm older, I am fully aware of the wide variety of manipulative tests women administer to men. When I was young and naïve though, I used to get played sometimes. I would be left feeling angry, confused, and frustrated. Slowly but surely, I became wise.

Reciprocators VS Pretenders:

"What if you meet a woman who initially gives every sign of being a Reciprocator? How can I distinguish her from a Pretender?"

Reciprocators do not look for incentives and rewards in exchange for their romantic and/or sexual companionship. If they are interested in communicating with you and sharing your company, they simply let you know.

A Pretender will usually make some sort of comment to you that lets you know that she is accustomed to being flattered by men, accommodated by men, wined & dined by men, and generally spoiled by men. If you bite on the manipulative bait, you are dead meat.

An interaction with a Reciprocator:

You: "I am very attracted to you, and I think we should share each other's company sometime in the near future . . ."
Desirable Woman: *"That sounds great."*
You: "Your place or mine?"
Desirable Woman: *"Yours."*
You: "Cool. I will call you before the week is over, and we will take it from there."

An interaction with a Pretender:

You: "I am very attracted to you, and I think we should share each other's company sometime in the near future . . ."

Desirable Woman: *"So what restaurant are we going to?"*

You: "Well, actually ... I was thinking more along the lines of a quiet, intimate evening at my place . . ."

Desirable Woman: *"Sorry, but I don't know you. I prefer to be taken out to lunch, dinner, a movie or a concert prior to going over to a man's residence. I don't know you like that."*

The latter is an example of a Pretender issuing one of her manipulative head games test. She will say she's just being "cautious." That is bullshit. If she was truly being cautious, she would invite you over to her place, and have a girlfriend there.

A Pretender is going to **always test you** to see what you are willing to offer her in exchange for her companionship. If not something monetary or tangible, at minimum something intangible such as a high degree of fawning and flattery.

Men, not that I'm trying to get you to watch adult films if that is not your thing, but you have to watch the opening scene in this movie entitled *Talk Dirty To Me*. I talk about this movie all of the time on message boards, blogs, and radio interviews. Adult film legend John Leslie stars as this incorrigible slacker womanizer named "Jack," and he has this interaction with this Wholesome Pretender type at the beginning of the film. The woman is this prim, proper, pretentious physician. How he breaks her down is just wonderful to watch.

One of his comments to her is, *"I bet most men would pay you big bucks to get in your pants, wouldn't they? Big bucks. (pause) Well, I wouldn't pay you SHIT."* I hollered with laughter when he said that. Sure enough, a few minutes later, she's on her knees giving him a blowjob. He passed her test, and he got rewarded for it.

Some might say, "Oh ... that's just a movie though." I beg to differ. I've had similar scenarios play out with me that unfolded just like that. When you are dealing with a Pretender type, you cannot give them the impression that you are willing to play **their game**. You cannot allow harsh criticisms to throw you for a loop, or allow threats of being indefinitely ignored cause you any sort of frustration.

The key with a Pretender is that you have to let them know that you value your own attention and companionship. If a woman thinks for a micro-second that you perceive her attention and companionship as more valuable than your own, she's going to toy with you until she gets bored, and then just unceremoniously dismiss you.

Men always ask, "What do the so-called Bad Boy types have to offer that the Nice Guy types in society do not have to offer?" Among other characteristics, the men who are perceived as Bad Boys **know their value** to women. Bad Boy types usually know that women find them exciting, edgy, intriguing, enigmatic, and challenging, so they have no pressing desire to "chase" women in an aggressive manner.

Nice Guy types are too quick to put women on pedestals. Bad Boys do not do that. They treat all women as if they have potential flaws and weaknesses in their behavior and their character. They treat all women as if they have a desire and/or need to be fucked. Nice Guys have a bad habit of treating women as if they are incapable of getting horny or incapable of entertaining erotic fantasies in their heads.

If you are breathing, you have the potential to get sexually aroused. The desire for sex is a natural part of every human being's makeup. With the possible exception of a priest or a nun, no man or woman can resist and/or suppress their lustful desires indefinitely.

Wholesome Pretenders VS Erotic Hypocrites

The two main types of Pretenders are Wholesome Pretenders (WPs) and Erotic Hypocrites (EHs). I talked about these two types of

87

women in Chapter Six of **Mode One**. In many ways, the two groups of women are just alike ... but they possess one or two differences.

Erotic Hypocrites are far more materialistic and social status-oriented than your average Wholesome Pretender. EHs usually target men with a high degree of career success, financial wealth, and middle class or upper class social status. WPs are simply women who like kinky sex and/or non-monogamous sex, but they don't want to ever be labeled a "whore/ho," a "slut," an "easy lay," or a "super freak."

EHs work similar to a high-priced Call Girl or Erotic Escort, but they would never officially want to be labeled as such. With some guys, the EH looks to exchange their sexual companionship for monetary favors, employment opportunities, and other tangible and intangible benefits that willing men are offering them.

A second scenario with an EH is to date and/or marry a man with means and status, but have side flings and affairs with Bad Boy types who don't have any wealth or status, but are really, really good in bed. I've seen this scenario play out with a number of women I've met over the years, particularly when I lived in Los Angeles.

WPs are women who like their sex raw, uninhibited, and kinky ... and to one degree or another ... they like having sex with a number of different partners ... but they want to give men who are the "marrying" type the public impression that they are very innocent, wholesome, virtuous and monogamous-minded.

WPs want to get married someday, but until they meet "Mr. Right," they want to enjoy as much kinky sexual pleasure as possible. A WP will initially frown on any casual sex proposition you throw at them. That is their "test." They love to have those "theatrical" reactions I spoke of earlier (e.g., *"Do you think I'm a ho? Think again Mister!"*)

Next time a Wholesome Pretender goes into "theatrical" mode, ask yourself this question: Why would anyone who is DENYING YOU something (i.e., romantic companionship, sexual companionship) be pissed off about it? Shouldn't **the one being rejected** be the one pissed instead of **the one <u>doing</u> the rejecting**? Think about that.

Let's take "Amber." Amber has engaged in a number of one-night stands, weekend flings, threesomes, and other variations of kinky sex, but Amber doesn't want "Mr. Nice Guy who might marry me someday" to know that. No way. That might cause this guy to perceive her as 'loose' and promiscuous. Amber doesn't want that.

So if Mr. Nice Guy was to approach Amber and even think about expressing an interest in only casual sex, Amber is going to let him

HAVE IT. *"What do I look like ... a slut to you? A two-bit whore?? You jerk!!!"* Mr. Nice Guy can't take those sorts of harsh criticisms. So he retracts his invitation for casual sex, and apologizes for his "rude" propositions. Just like Amber wants and expects him to. Amber is smiling. In her mind, she is like "What a weak ass punk. I made him back down. I am so bad!!!"

Next up, a Mode One / Bad Boy type. Just like Mr. Nice Guy, he expresses an interest in only casual sex as well. Amber, once again, says, *"What do I look like ... a slut to you? A two-bit whore? You jerk!!"* Amber smirks to herself, expecting an apology and a retraction. To her surprise, Mr. Mode One doesn't offer either.

Mr. Mode One just looks her dead in her eyes and smirks himself. "You must be really horny. I can sense that you're tense and sexually frustrated...." Amber is trippin'. That's not the response she was expecting to hear. Mr. Mode One Guy continues. "I don't know if I'll have time to exchange orgasms with you this week ... but we'll hook up in two or three weeks. I'm sure of that." Cocky bastard.

Amber can't figure this guy out. *"Did this guy already talk to one of my ex-lovers?"* she thinks in her mind. *"Did he talk to one of my girlfriends who I share my sexual secrets with?"* she ponders. *"Why is he so confident that he can break me down?"* she wonders.

90

Mr. Mode One Guy doesn't really know her history. He doesn't know her "M.O." He knows what he wants, and he doesn't apologize for it. He knows he only wants casual sex, and nothing else is even on the table as an option. Why should he ever apologize for truth?

Soon, Amber lightens up and gives in to the conversation. Hours later, days later, or weeks later, Amber is in bed with Mr. Mode One Guy. Your classic Wholesome Pretender. Mr. Mode One passed Amber's manipulative test(s) and he is rewarded for it.

You see men, you can't break down a Rejecter (don't even try to), but you can surely break down an Erotic Hypocrite and/or a Wholesome Pretender. The key is **knowing what you want** from those women and never wavering from that. Don't ever apologize for being upfront, straightforward and truthful. No need to.

Remember: A Pretender is a woman who has some degree of attraction and interest in you, but she's always going to 'play the role' in order to protect her image and reputation. Very few women, particularly women under thirty-five who have never been married, want to ever risk developing a "questionable" reputation (I have found that most older women and/or women who have already been married once or twice really don't give a damn how you perceive them. They just live their life).

Don't try to play games with a Pretender. You will lose. An EH or a WP will have you for dinner if you engage in head games with them. These two types of women know how to take advantage of a guy who is 'pretending' themselves (i.e., A guy who is pretending not to be after sex, but really is). These women are professionals and prey on men who are weak with no balls and no real backbone.

With an EH or WP, you have to express your desires and interests to them in a bold, to-the-point, totally unapologetic manner. You have to talk to a WP as if you already have factual knowledge that she has engaged in kinky, non-monogamous casual sex and she enjoyed it. Even if in reality, you don't know anything about this woman.

I tell men all of the time: It is always better to approach a woman who is a genuine "good girl" type with the assumption that she is a "kinky freak" type than it is to be guilty of vice versa. I've never regretted treating a good girl like a freak, but I've always regretted treating a WP like an innocent, wholesome, virtuous good girl.

Casual sex is the 800 pound gorilla in society. We go around behaving as though no one is engaging in casual sex, when the reality is, practically everyone is engaging in some form of casual sex. Be real about it. People need to quit being phony, duplicitous and hypocritical about their sexual desires.

It's amazing the lengths some men and women will go to protect their so-called "innocent, wholesome, conservative" image and reputation. Have you by chance seen a film entitled *Eyes Wide Shut*? This is a movie starring Tom Cruise and his ex-wife Nicole Kidman, and directed by the legendary Stanley Kubrick. Good, good film.

One of the subplots of the film involves Cruise's character, Dr. Bill Harford, sneaking into a highly exclusive swinging party with a number of wealthy, powerful high society types. When it is discovered that Dr. Harford wasn't on the official invite list, not only is he forced to leave, but his life literally becomes endangered. Why?

Because the folk who attended this kinky party don't want any strangers putting their image and reputation at risk. These folk want their "secret activities," which include very unconventional, kinky sex acts, to remain absolutely private. And these are folk with Venetian Carnival masks on (Once you watch *Eyes Wide Shut*, the sound of that piano playing will haunt you). Real life baby.

Even with all sorts of STDs floating around, men and women will always have some degree of desire to engage in premarital sex and casual sex. That is just the nature of the times we live in.

Questions:

1) If you are a woman reading this, do you often "pretend" as if you have no interest in casual sex, when you know deep-down that you love casual sex? If so, do you give men "theatrical" reactions to prevent them from perceiving you as an "easy lay," a "ho," or a "kinky slut?"

2) If you are a woman reading this, do you expect to be wined & dined in exchange for letting a woman have sex with you? Do you use your sexual companionship as a means of motivating men to offer you financial favors and employment opportunities?

3) If you are a man reading this, do you frequently flatter women and/or offer women financial favors in an attempt to get them in bed?

4) If you are a man reading this, when you want to have casual sex with a woman, do you let her know in an upfront and straightforward manner? Or do you "pretend" as though you are only looking for a long-term monogamous relationship?

Chapter EIGHT

Timewasters

Welcome back ladies. Sorry I had to ignore you in Chapter Seven, but again, there are just really not any males who exhibit the behavior of a Pretender. If a man is interested in having casual sex with a woman, and he knows that a woman he is attracted to is interested in the same thing, that man is not going to pretend not to be interested.

On the other hand, men surely know how to pretend to have the same interests as a woman, when they really do not. This is exactly what a Timewaster is. Anytime you meet a man or woman, and that person is initially behaving as though they have the same exact romantic and/or sexual desires and interests as you, but in reality, they have a totally different, underlying agenda … that is representative of a Timewaster's behavior. This is their "M.O."

Timewasters are many times mistaken for and confused with Reciprocators because they will almost always respond to you initially in an enthusiastic, friendly, reciprocal manner. The reality is, Timewasters are more similar to a Rejecter. A Pretender is nothing more than the manipulative version of a Reciprocator, and a

Timewaster is nothing more than the manipulative version of a Rejecter. Pretenders and Timewasters love to play head games.

The typical female Timewaster is a woman who temporarily or indefinitely pretends to have some sort of romantic and/or sexual attraction to you, but deep-down, they see you as nothing beyond someone to receive financial favors from, flattering attention from, entertaining companionship from, or if nothing else, simply a listening ear when they want to vent.

The most common form of male Timewasters are those men who temporarily or indefinitely pretend as though they have an interest in the same sort of long-term monogamous relationship that you have already expressed an interest in, but in reality, they just want short-term monogamous sex, short-term non-monogamous sex, or long-term non-monogamous sex.

Another variation of a male Timewaster would be a man who indefinitely pretends to behave like your "play brother" or "friendly neighbor or co-worker," but in reality, he wants to get in a woman's pants. As I mentioned on page 45, this is what I commonly refer to as the art of "**FunClubbing**." A good friend and fraternity brother of mine created that term when I was in college. He said, "Alan ...

make sure you never join a woman's 'Fun Club.' You will only end up frustrated at the end."

My friend went on to say that a woman's "Fun Club" is her stable of male platonic friends who keep her entertained, flatter her ego and give a boost to her confidence and self-esteem when needed, and listen to her vent about ex-boyfriends and ex-lovers who have caused her pain and frustration. The problem is, all of these "platonic friends" really want to date this woman or have [casual] sex with her.

In Chapter Seven, I described the main two types of Pretenders (both female) which are "Erotic Hypocrites" and "Wholesome Pretenders." Now I am going to describe the various types of Timewasters.

General Types of Women who tend to be Timewasters

<u>Attention Whores, Dick Teasers, Exploiters and Users</u>

If there is one thing you will very rarely see a man do, it is dress 'sexy' or behave in a sexually provocative manner towards a woman just to get flattering attention. Women, trust me on this: If a man exhibits erotic or sexually provocative behavior towards a woman, nine times out of ten, he wants to exchange orgasms with that woman.

ALAN ROGER CURRIE

Women are a different breed in this respect. Many women will wear sexy clothes and behave in a flirtatious, sexually provocative manner just to receive *flattering attention*. Speaking for the vast majority of men, we cannot relate to that. The average man would rather have a blowjob than a flattering compliment any day. I once had a woman tell me that she wanted to be a centerfold selection in *Playboy* magazine simply so she could feel desired and receive more compliments from men. Again, as a man, I cannot relate to that.

Women who use their feminine charms and sex appeal for the primary purpose of receiving flattering attention and compliments are generally known as "Attention Whores" and/or "Dick Teasers." Attention Whores and Dick Teasers motivate men to give them attention by giving these men the subtle impression of, "If you flatter me and give me the type of attention I want, I might just let you sleep with me one day soon…" Think of the ultra-seductive character of "Ginger" (Tina Louise) from the 60s television show, Gilligan's Island.

Another variation of a female Timewaster is the "Exploiter" and/or "User." These manipulative game players don't want flattering attention or entertaining companionship as much as they want monetary favors, materialistic gifts, employment offers, and other benefits which are more tangible in nature.

98

How can you usually distinguish between a [female] Timewaster and a [female] Reciprocator? With a Reciprocator, the woman's words and actions will be congruent with one another. There will be no inconsistencies or contradictions between her words, her body language and overall behavior. With a Timewaster, if you are observant and perceptive enough, you will quickly see inconsistencies and contradictions between the woman's words, body language and overall behavior.

A Timewaster's words will say, *"Yes, I am interested in dating you and having sex with you at some point ...,"* but their actions and behavior will be saying, *"Please don't get too close to me. I am not attracted to you at all."*

Some men don't mind the behavior of Timewasters. I know men who would rather share the company of a female Timewaster than no woman at all (usually a Mode Three type guy or even a Mode Two type guy). Not a Mode One type guy. A Mode One type guy would rather be indefinitely single and by himself than share the company of a Timewaster on a monthly, weekly, or daily basis.

Most erotic strippers are nothing more than paid Timewasters. 90% of all strippers are not going to have sex with you. You pay them to dick tease you. You pay them to show you their sexy side and their naked bodies. If you are good with that, cool. As you can sense, I am not the biggest fan of strip clubs. I'm not into being erotically teased with no chance of exchanging orgasms with that particular woman.

General Types of Men who tend to be Timewasters

<u>Dogs and Lying Womanizers</u>

As mentioned briefly in Chapter Three, there are some guys who are straight-up "Players." A Player is a guy who maintains two, three or more different sex partners, but all of these women have full knowledge that he is having sex with other women. The women are cool with this scenario.

There are other men though who want to have multiple sex partners, but because of their profound fear of rejection (Mode Three) and/or fear of harsh criticism (Mode Two), they begin to get into a habit of lying to women, misleading women, and generally manipulating women. These men have yet to grow a real set of balls.

These men are typically known as "Dogs" and/or "Lying Womanizers." If a Lying Womanizer has three or four different sex partners, you can bet money that each of those women are under the misguided belief that she is this guy's only sex partner.

Dogs and Lying Womanizers don't have the cojones to be upfront and straightforwardly honest about their true desire for non-monogamous sex with a multiplicity of female sex partners. Bi-sexual "Down Low" men fall into this category too. Lying is commonplace.

You see, a Player type knows his popularity is high and his sex skills are above-average, if not exceptional. Therefore, he has no fear of rejection. He knows many women won't mind sharing him with other women. I respect a true Player type. He has integrity.

Dogs and Lying Womanizers have no character or integrity regarding how they handle women. They tell lies on top of other lies. If a Dog or Lying Womanizer type gets a 'serious girlfriend' or wife, there is a 99.999999% chance he is going to cheat on her. Regularly.

As a woman, how can you identify a Dog or Lying Womanizer? Simple. Watch how he interacts with other women. Does he flirt a lot in a physical and sexually provocative manner? Is he enthusiastic about taking you out in public and showing you off? Does he always want to just come over to your place or have you come over to his?

Dogs and Lying Womanizers do not want to be seen with you in public, unless you are his main girlfriend, fiancée, or wife.

Some women are cool with being a man's mistress, or #2, #3, or #4 sex partner. If that works for you as a woman, more power to you.

Playboys and Serial Monogamists

There are some men who just want as much sex from women as they can possibly get. Those guys are usually incorrigible womanizers who more so fall into the category of a "Dog" and/or "Lying Womanizer." With these guys, it's all about pure quantity of women.

Then there are other guys who put more emphasis on the **quality** of women they are having sex with rather than the quantity. This is when you run into your Playboys and Serial Monogamists.

These men qualify for the title of "Timewaster" because usually, they are looking for short-term sex from women who would much prefer to be involved in a long-term monogamous relationship that is going to ultimately lead to marriage. These men rarely flat-out lie to women, but their behavior and actions are definitely *misleading*, to say the least.

With a Playboy or Serial Monogamist, they are not looking to bed as many women as possible in a short period of time. These men go after women who are attractive and well-groomed; women who carry themselves in a classy manner; women who are generally intelligent and probably college educated; and many times, women who enjoy a high degree of career success and financial stability.

To their credit, these guys are not looking to just abuse women and treat them like shallow sex objects. Men in this category are not looking for a one-night stand or a weekend fling. They want a monogamous sexual relationship with each woman they pursue.

The problem is, they desire a relationship that won't last as long as the type of relationship the women who they are pursuing desire. For example, you might have "Peter" who is looking to have monogamous sex with "Dayna" for anywhere from six weeks to six months; Dayna on the other hand wants a long-term monogamous relationship that will potentially result in her and Peter getting married. Peter is not trying to put a ring on Dayna's finger.

The upside for most women who deal with men in this category is that these men will be romantic, attentive, caring, and respectful. These men will not be running around with five other different women on the side. These men genuinely enjoy your company.

The issue is simply a matter of "for how long?" Plain and simply, Playboys and Serial Monogamists really don't want to be married.

These men do not want to be 'tied down' to one woman for a long number of years. They want the freedom to meet and date a number of different women over the years of their adult life.

Legendary feature-film actor Warren Beatty is an example of a man who was known for years (if not decades) in Hollywood as a Serial Monogamist. Women rarely, if ever, categorized Beatty as a "Dog" or a "Lying Womanizer," because that wasn't really his M.O.

Beatty would treat women with the highest degree of love, respect and discretion. He just wouldn't propose marriage to these women. Finally, Annette Bening got him to propose. And the Serial Monogamist finally settled down (I'm a huge Warren Beatty fan).

If you are a woman, and you are specifically looking to get married, the men in this category are going to disappoint you, if not flat-out crush your heart. Your best bet is not to have sex with these men until you are confident that they are going to put a ring on your finger. I realize that is easier said thandone for many women, but that is pretty much the only way of protecting yourself from the emotional frustration of a short lived romantic relationship.

The first sign that a man is a Playboy or Serial Monogamist relates to my advice in the paragraph above. These men will not hold out too long for sex. If you make a Serial Monogamist wait a couple of weeks, or even a month or so, no problem. You make a Serial Monogamist wait three months, six months, nine months or longer … nine times out of ten, he is history. He is then on to the next woman.

FunClubbers, Mode Three Targets, and Weasels

Have you ever heard the term or phrase, "that guy is trying to weasel his way into that woman's pants!"? A man who is a Weasel uses probably the oldest manipulative trick in the book: Attempting to have sex with a woman by pretending that he is doing everything **but** trying to have sex with a woman.

This is also what men who are "Mode Three Targets" (defined in my *Mode One* book) and FunClubbers do. Their objective is to indefinitely pretend to be content with a non-physical, non-sexual relationship … or "friendship" … while they hold out hoping for that one day when the woman might be vulnerable and/or horny.

Of the three categories of male Timewasters … Dogs/Lying Womanizers, Playboys/Serial Monogamists, and FunClubbers/Mode Three Targets/Weasels, I would have to say I have met more men who fall into the latter category than any of the other two.

I just told a high school classmate of mine this recently. I told her that there are many men who will pretend to be "just friends" with a woman for two years, three years, five years, seven years, even ten or more years just to patiently wait for one opportunity to get in that woman's pants. These guys literally want just **one opportunity** to exchange orgasms with a woman of interest. Now that is patience.

A woman who is an Attention Whore or Dick Teaser will love interacting with a man who is a FunClubber or Weasel. A woman who is an Exploiter or User will love interacting with a man who is a Mode Three Target (when you really think about it, most of the male and female manipulative game players tend to match up well with one another ... Erotic Hypocrites with Playboys/Serial Monogamists; Wholesome Pretenders with Dogs/Lying Womanizers; and of course, the aforementioned match-ups).

The major strength, of course, of men in this category is their indefinite sense of patience. Men who are Dogs and Lying Womanizers usually cannot wait too long before making attempts to have sex with a woman. Men who are Playboys and Serial Monogamists typically have more patience than the average Dog or Lying Womanizer, but they do not have as much patience as the average FunClubber, Mode Three Target or Weasel.

The FunClubber is the guy who is willing to be a woman's "play brother" indefinitely. This man is almost like a woman's "platonic boyfriend." He will go to the movies with a woman, talk on the phone regularly with her, go grocery shopping with her, go to parties and social events with her, all of that. Some women might say, *"Alan, that simply sounds like a good, well-intentioned platonic male friend to me!!"* Close. The big difference between a FunClubber and a genuine platonic male friend is his suppressed romantic and/or sexual desires and interests. A true male friend has no hidden agenda.

If a man was a genuine platonic friend, then even if his female friend offered him sex, he wouldn't take it. He would refuse any invitation for sexual interplay. A FunClubber would jump at the chance to have sex if a woman offered him the opportunity, but he would never boldly ask her for sexual companionship. That would put him at risk of being harshly criticized and/or rejected. No balls for that.

The Weasel is similar to the FunClubber, but he is a wee bit more calculating and far more disingenuous. The Weasel doesn't simply wait around with his fingers crossed. The Weasel usually has a strategic plan to get in between a woman's legs. He plans the opportunity for sex in the same manner that an event planner takes step-by-step actions in preparation for that one big event on his or her calendar.

The Weasel's plan might be to get the woman drunk one night, and then take advantage of her, or it might be to pop a porno DVD in her DVD player when she is not looking. It might even be as extreme as drugging her with an Ecstasy pill.

<u>Side Note</u>: In 2007 I had a group of older church-going women encourage me to go on a high school and college tour to tell young men ages fifteen to twenty-two or twenty-three to have the balls to exhibit Mode One Behavior and risk being rejected then to get girls sloppy drunk and/or put Ecstasy pills in their drinks in an attempt to date rape the girls without their consent. I think such behavior by any man is shameful and deplorable. I can't tell you what I would do if I found out a young man drugged a daughter of mine in his cowardly attempt to have sex with her.

The Mode Three Target is also similar to a FunClubber, with the only difference being that he will dish out more money, more financial favors, and more materialistic gifts than a FunClubber will.   The Mode Three Target will do a lot of wining and dining of women … he will buy them inexpensive and even many times expensive gifts … he will help the women with bills and living expenses … pay for trips … but the whole time, he will pretend like he's just being "nice" and generous with no strings attached. Yeah … RIGHT.

Men who are Mode Three Targets are dreadfully afraid of being rejected, ignored or feeling lonely. They always want female companionship. I have met some men who literally cannot go more than two or three days without female companionship, even if the companionship is not romantic, physical, or sexual.

If you are a woman, and you suspect a man of being a FunClubber, Mode Three Target, or Weasel type, the best thing to do is simply to ask him straightforwardly, *"Do you want to have sex with me? Sometimes, I get the feeling you want to have sex with me, and I just want to clarify things between us."* See what his response is.

If you are a woman with manipulative tendencies, you will never, ever ask that question. Never. If you are a non-manipulative woman, it would be to your benefit to ask that question to eliminate potential "drama" later on down the line.

Timewasters, in the long-run, can cause you more anger, frustration, bitterness, and emotional pain than a Rejecter or Pretender ever will. Men do not like to waste time and/or money and not have it lead to anything beneficial or satisfying. Women do not like to have their emotions toyed with and have their hearts broken. Women look to avoid wasteful emotional investments in the same way men look to avoid wasteful financial investments.

How much Timewasters affect you depends a lot on your age. When you are young (teenage years, your twenties, early-to-mid thirties), you do not value time as much as you do when you are thirty-five and older. When I was nineteen or twenty, I actually didn't mind 'wasting time' with women because I really didn't see it as that big of a deal.

When I reached my early-to-mid thirties, I began to absolutely hate wasting time with women who didn't share the same romantic and/or sexual interests as me. I will take a Rejecter over a Timewaster any day. This is why I tell men all of the time: Don't trip out over rejection. Rejection is necessary and inevitable.

Questions:

1) If you are a woman, do you like to have men think about you in a sexual manner just so you can get them to flatter you and/or provide you with entertaining companionship?

2) Similar to Question #1, do you hold the opportunity for sex with you as a "carrot on a stick" to men to motivate them to provide you with financial favors, materialistic gifts, and employment opportunities?

3) If you are a man, do you often pretend to be interested in monogamous sex when you know deep-down that you really want non-monogamous sex? Do you pretend to be interested in a long-term relationship when you really want a relationship that will last no more than a few weeks or a few months?

4) If you are a man, do you often pretend to be content with a "platonic" friendship with a woman when you know good and well that you want something romantic and/or sexual with your "good female friend?" Why do you do this?

5) When you felt like your time was wasted, did you feel angry?

Chapter NINE

Are You REALLY Tired of Manipulative Head Games?

I hear a lot of men and women say, "I am so tired of games," but I am very skeptical towards many when I hear them say this. I believe many men and women love to engage in head games with members of the opposite sex mainly because they are very, very good at it.

If you read *Mode One*, you know that I feel there are two primary factors that motivate manipulative game playing: **1)** Fear and **2)** Spoiled Egos. When you are afraid of being rejected, being ignored, and/or being harshly criticized, this is when you tend to employ manipulative tactics to get what you want. Secondly, when you are so spoiled and used to getting your way that you can't fathom not having your way, you tend to become manipulative.

I don't think your love life, sex life and/or social life will ever truly be enjoyable and satisfying as long as you are allowing men or women to mislead you and manipulate you. Remember: No one can truly manipulate you unless you're trying to manipulate them. If you're not trying to mislead and manipulate others, then the only other way you can be manipulated is if you are just really, really naïve.

It cracks me up to hear manipulative game players always use the defense, *"Don't judge me!!"* when you call them out on their manipulative tactics and tendencies. A friend and I were just talking about this. That comment is without question the #1 patented response to accusations of being manipulative. ***"Don't judge me!!"***

Yes, I am going to judge you. Not by my standards, not by GOD's standards or biblical standards, not by your mother or father's standards, but more so by **your own standards**.

I believe one of the first things you should do when you start interacting with a man or woman who you are attracted to is to find out what are their standards and principles for their own behavior, and what are their general expectations for those they plan on dating or having [casual] sex with. For example . . .

• What are your thoughts on monogamy versus non-monogamy?

• How much do you value honesty in a relationship?

• What role does sex play in your level of happiness in a relationship?

• What role does money and financial security play in your level of happiness in a relationship?

• Has anyone ever betrayed your trust, and if so, how did that make you feel? Have you ever betrayed someone else's trust, and if so, did you feel regretful later on?

It's been said that if you want the right answers, you have to ask the right questions. There are a number of questions you can ask a potential boyfriend, girlfriend or casual sex lover, but the questions I listed are fundamental and much needed to establish what that person's standards are for their own behavior.

Then, when they violate their own standards, you can say to them, "I'm judging you by the standards you set for yourself." It is very rare when I pass judgment on other people's dating and sex habits based on my own personal, opinionated standards.

If you are a man who is bi-sexual ... I don't care. Just be upfront and straightforward with the women you date and have sex with. If you are into polyamorous dating and maintaining a multiplicity of sex partners ... that is on you. Just be upfront and straightforward with the men and women you date and choose to have sex with. My thing is, whatever your romantic and/or sexual desires are, just have the cojones to be upfront and straightforward about them.

It is funny how some men and women will stop engaging in manipulative head games when their tools for manipulation begin to diminish. If a woman's primary manipulative tool was her looks and sex appeal, as soon as she becomes old, fat, and unattractive, all of the sudden you will hear the former master manipulator say, "I hate games." Same with a man who used to have a high degree of career success, wealth and material possessions. Now that he's unemployed, damn near broke, and no materialistic 'toys' to brag about, all of the sudden he says, "I hate women who play games." Too funny.

Developing an interpersonal communication style that is upfront and straightforward is not easy. It takes work and practice. Repetition, repetition, repetition. If it were easy, everyone would communicate in an upfront and straightforward manner with one another.

"I have no interest in dating that man, but I don't have the heart to tell him. Maybe I will just ignore his Email messages and phone calls." So ... you're scared of hurting the guy's feelings huh? Well, let's see here. You think blatantly not returning his phone calls gives his ego and feelings a boost? You believe that simply not responding to his Email messages makes him feel good about himself?

"The woman I met is not really my type for marriage or long-term dating. I just want to have a few days or a few weeks of casual sex with her. If I tell her that though, it will make me look shallow." So, you don't have the balls to tell the woman upfront that you just want to exchange orgasms with her huh? Well, let's see here. You believe that misleading a woman into believing that you genuinely care for her and sincerely enjoy spending time with her, when in reality you

only want to experience the joy of shooting out baby batter, is the best way to go? Think about that for a moment. I mean, really.

No one reading this book would want a man toying with their mother's feelings, or taking advantage of their beloved father's financial generosity. Why then would YOU want to mislead others?

Always invite people to be straightforwardly honest with you. Even if what they say is not what your ego wants to hear. When you attach negative connotations and/or consequences to straightforward honesty, most people will resort back to lying and manipulation.

I'm particularly talking to the women. If a man approaches you, and lets you know that all he wants to do is have a one-night stand or a weekend fling, don't pass judgment on his desires simply because they are not in line with yours. Simply say, *"Casual sex is not my cup of tea, but I appreciate your honesty."*

If you get "theatrical" with this guy, he is going to return to lying and manipulation (if you are manipulative yourself, you really don't care).

In the next chapter, I will answer some common questions associated with Mode One Behavior.

Questions:

1) How has engaging in manipulative head games benefited you as a man or a woman? Do you have any motivation to stop engaging in manipulative head games?

2) Do you see anything wrong with manipulative head games?

3) When you meet a man or woman you want to date or have casual sex with, what are some of the questions you ask your potential companions and potential lovers? What are some of the questions that they ask you? Do you answer those questions honestly? If not, why?

Chapter TEN

Frequently Asked Questions

When I'm on many blogs, message boards, and discussion forums, such as *AskMen.com* and *Direct-Method.com*, I'm asked a number of questions from both men and women, as well those who have already read Mode One and those who have not. In this chapter, I will attempt to answer most of the more common questions I receive.

"Isn't Mode One just another get-laid-quick scheme for men who perceive themselves as 'losers' to suddenly get a few women in bed so they can feel like successful womanizers?"

My reply: I've never thought of the Mode One mindset as a 'method' or 'technique' for the sole and specific purpose of seducing women and getting laid. Matter of fact, I tell men all of the time … if your only reason for wanting to exhibit Mode One Behavior with women is to become an 'overnight womanizer,' then nine times out of ten, you are going to feel disappointed and frustrated in the long-run.

If I had to use a baseball analogy, Mode One is about teaching a potential home run hitter how to get over his fear of striking out. All home run hitters have a high degree of strike outs. It's just part of the game. Same with approaching, attracting and seducing women. You will never be successful with women if you are dreadfully afraid of being rejected and/or harshly criticized.

Being upfront and straightforward with the opposite sex is not a 'scheme.' It is a lifestyle and a constant mindset you must maintain.

"If being Mode One with women is all about straightforward honesty, then how come I can't just walk up to a woman I don't know and say 'I want you to give me a blowjob!' Wouldn't that be representative of straightforward honesty if that is what I'm REALLY thinking?"

<u>My reply</u>: This is what I tell men when I'm asked questions similar to this one: You can say ANYTHING you want to a woman as long as you are prepared to accept the potential consequences and/or repercussions of what you say.

In other words, there is a fine line difference between being bold, self-assured, upfront and unapologetically straightforward … and being stupid and foolish. You have to be experienced enough to know where that line is. Think before you speak.

Trust me ... I have approached women and opened up the conversation with some very bold, XXX-rated, sexually provocative comments ... and 90% of the time, it has worked in my favor ... but the key is, I know how to read women's body language and quickly size up what type of woman I'm dealing with (e.g., self-righteous prude type, kinky freak type, Wholesome Pretender type, etc).

If you are a man, you have to spend days, weeks, and months just studying women. This is what I did in my twenties and early thirties. I would literally go to nightclubs and other social venues just to study women's nuances, body language and behavioral tendencies.

In the long-run, that studying pays off.

"I am very confident about approaching women when they are by themselves, but I am dreadfully afraid to approach women when they are with one, two or three of their girlfriends. Any advice?"

My reply: I don't like to approach women when they are in a group unless I absolutely have to. Women will rarely behave in a real, authentic manner when they are with their girlfriends. They will 'play the role.' They will exhibit the behavior that their girlfriends have come to expect of them.

For example, if a woman is a kinky freak behind-closed-doors, but she gives all of her girlfriends the misleading impression that she is a conservative prude type, you're going to have a very challenging time getting her to drop that façade in front of her girlfriends.

What I do in group situations is find a way to get the woman away from her girlfriends so I can talk to her one-on-one. That usually works much better. "Cock blocking" happens a lot in groups.

"Does the Four Modes of Verbal Communication™ apply to single women as much as it applies to single men?"

<u>My reply</u>: My answer would almost simultaneously be "yes" ... and "no." Read my chapter on "Pretenders." There really are no male Pretenders *(i.e., men who share the same romantic and/or sexual interests as you, but will pretend not to)*. There are many male Timewasters *(i.e., men who do not share the same desires and interests as you, but will indefinitely pretend to)*, so Mode One Behavior could be used by a woman to identify those types.

Women do not approach men as much as vice versa, so some of the psychology behind the Four Modes of Verbal Communication™ just would not apply in the exact same manner. I have had many women who have wrote me and told me that reading Mode One has helped them understand men a lot more though. That's always a plus.

"I always read where you sing the praises of a porno movie entitled 'Talk Dirty To Me,' and the lead character 'Jack.' What was so special about that movie and that character? Aren't all adult films generally the same? Sex, sex and more sex?"

<u>My reply</u>: **Talk Dirty To Me** starring adult film legend John Leslie as "Jack" was the very first impetus for the development of the Four Modes of Verbal Communication™. For starters, I never knew what a "Wholesome Pretender" was before I saw that film.

Watching that film was when I first really learned about women's sexual duplicity (i.e., a woman pretending to be 'innocent' and 'wholesome' when in reality, she is erotically uninhibited and/or into non-monogamous sex). Secondly, the character of Jack taught me how to ignore harsh, subjective criticisms and opinionated insults.

Even if you take the explicit sex scenes out of **Talk Dirty To Me** and the sequel, **Talk Dirty To Me, Part II** ... and converted those movies from XXX-rated to R-rated, they would still be great movies and very educational to watch. Those movies could easily be re-named "Wholesome Pretenders, Part 1" and "Wholesome Pretenders, Part 2."

I actually plan on filming a DVD entitled "Pretenders and Timewasters" sometime soon. I will keep my book readers posted.

"Why do you emphasize identifying manipulators so much? Why isn't your book more about attraction and seduction techniques than manipulation between the sexes?"

<u>My reply</u>: The ability to attract and seduce the opposite sex varies from man to man and from woman to woman. Therefore, I don't really put too much emphasis on "Dating 101" guidelines or "Seduction 101" tips, tricks and techniques.

It is doubtful that the same principles that help Black men attract Black women would also help Caucasian men attract Caucasian women or Asian men attract Asian women. It is doubtful that the principles that would help an eighteen or nineteen year-old college fraternity guy would be the same principles that would help a blue-collar factory worker who is between forty-five and fifty-nine.

A lot of helpful, valid dating and seduction advice really depends to a large degree on how old you are, what your physical appearance is like, your level of intelligence and education, your level of career success and financial success, how good you are in bed, etc.

Many so-called "experts" and "gurus" will have you foolishly believing that dating advice is "one philosophy fits all." That is so untrue. My ability to attract and seduce women in their thirties was totally different than my ability to attract and seduce women between the ages of seventeen and twenty-four.

Manipulation on the other hand is, for the most part, universal. I don't care if you are nineteen, twenty-nine, thirty-nine or forty-nine, you can relate equally to the concept of manipulative head games.

"Why do so many women pretend to be only into monogamous sex when they are really into non-monogamous casual sex?"

<u>My reply</u>: Plain and simply, most women are dreadfully afraid of being labeled a 'slut,' a 'whore,' an 'easy lay' or a 'super freak.' Women value their sense of virtue in the same way that most men value their sense of manhood and machismo.

Women love sex as much or more than most men do, but they love the idea of maintaining a good reputation that is beyond reproach even more. Women are especially this way if they are looking to get married and/or have children. The reality of life is women who are kinky and/or promiscuous often times get married just as frequently as the so-called "good girls."

"Why do men cheat and commit adultery so much? Why can't men just find a good woman and remain faithful to her?"

<u>My reply</u>: It is my belief that very few men are truly motivated to maintain a monogamous sexual relationship with one woman for the rest of their lives ... particularly if they are handsome, charming, wealthy, and/or have a number of attractive, sexy women throwing themselves at them.

All of us are guided primarily by four factors: Our desires and impulses, our fears and insecurities, our morals, values and principles, and our past experiences. If a man has a desire to have sex with a wide variety of women, the only thing that is going to stop him from acting on that desire or impulse is **a)** some sort of fear or insecurity (e.g., the fear of losing his wife and family; the insecurity that he is not really good in bed); **b)** his morals, values and/or principles (e.g., devout Christian, Doesn't believe in betraying the trust of others, etc); or **c)** a bad past experience (e.g., one of his former girlfriends cheated on him and it was emotionally painful for him).

If none of those factors come into play, then a man is left with nothing but his desires and impulses. This is what happens with mentally ill people such as serial killers. Serial killers operate on their desires and impulses. Their fears and insecurities are diminished, they virtually have no morals, values and principles, and their past experiences usually involve trauma, abuse, or profound disrespect and ill treatment.

You have to be fair and objective though. Women cheat on their boyfriends, fiancés, and husbands just as much as men cheat on their girlfriends, fiancées, and wives. Many men and women ... you guessed it ... PRETEND ... to be interested in a monogamous relationship when in actuality, they enjoy non-monogamy.

"What is so wrong with a man being a 'nice guy' or a 'gentleman?' Why do you have to be an 'asshole' or a 'jerk' in order to attract women?"

My reply: The main problem with men who try to be "Mr. Nice Guy" types is that they make the frequent mistake of putting women on pedestals, and trying too hard to prevent and/or avoid negative reactions and harsh criticisms. Read page 51 in *Mode One*.

A 'gentleman' in my book is someone who has respect for women, and is just the opposite of a misogynist. To be a 'gentleman' though is not necessarily synonymous with being a 'nice guy.' The movie character of *James Bond* is a 'gentleman,' but he is still smooth, debonair and an incorrigible womanizer.

"If I want to have a threesome with a woman I know and her best friend, should I just ask her? Or is that too forward or too bold?"

My reply: What can she do ... kill you? Ask. The worst she can say is, *"Have you lost your fu**in' mind?!?"* No, I'm kidding. Obviously, you did not see the Woody Allen romantic comedy, *Vicky Cristina Barcelona*. In that delightful film (actress *Penélope Cruz* won an Academy Award for her role in this movie), the character of Juan Antonio Gonzalo (Javier Bardem being Mode One) did just that. He let two women who were good friends (Vicky and Cristina) know that he wanted to have a threesome with them. A desire is a desire.

"I am a woman who is looking for a man who is financially secure who I don't have to take care of. Some men mistake me for a gold digger. I'm not looking for any man to take care of me ... I just don't want to play 'sugar mama' to them. How do I prevent men from mistaking me for a common gold digger?"

My reply: If you are a woman who has a successful career and earning a high five-figure salary or six-figure salary, there is nothing wrong with you looking for a romantic companion who is "on your level." If that means some men will refer to you as a 'gold digger,' so be it. Never allow other peoples perceptions of you and/or opinionated labels dictate how you behave towards others.

"Alan, you say that rejection is not that big of a deal, but what if you are a man who has not had a date in three or four years? What if your options for female companionships are limited? Isn't it then harder to deal with rejection?

<u>My reply</u>: If you are a man who has not socially interacted with a woman in over two or three years, then you need to really ask yourself why is that the case.

Do you have personal hygiene problems? Are you obese? Are your social skills just really, really horrible? Take an assessment of what you have to offer to women, and what areas of your life might warrant improvement.

If you need to improve your physical appearance, change your diet and your exercise habits. If you need to improve your social skills, then involve yourself in some personal development and self-improvement seminars. If you need to move to a new city, state, and/or country to meet more women … do it! You only live once.

Don't engage in "self-pity parties." Rejection by one woman simply brings you closer to the women you are supposed to be interacting with. Build a strategy for yourself and act on it.

Chapter ELEVEN

One Game You CAN Play
with Members of the Opposite Sex

I'll call this "The Mode One Game." The purpose is to help single men improve their interpersonal communication skills, their sense of self-confidence, and their ability to read a woman's body language.

The game requires at least one single man (there can be more than one involved), and preferably a minimum of four single women. If necessary, it could be switched around (one or more women with four or more men), but it is mainly designed to help the single men.

The only props you need are index cards, a pen or pencil, and a timer or stopwatch. The game will work the best if you have at least four different rooms in a house to work with. You can even put a little "monetary wager" on this game to make it more interesting.

Here is how the game will unfold:

The four or more women will go into a room by themselves and decide what woman will play what "role." The man (or men) involved in the game cannot have any prior knowledge of what woman is going to play what role. Here are the roles (should have enough women to play no less than four of these roles):

1) **Woman #1** is interested in a long-term monogamous relationship that will ultimately lead to marriage. Her behavior will be pretty straightforward with the man (or men) involved with the game.

2) **Woman #2** prefers a long-term monogamous relationship that will ultimately lead to marriage, but she is willing to settle for a long-term non-monogamous relationship that is full of enjoyable and satisfying sex. Woman #2 will never reveal her true desires and interests easily or straightforwardly.

3) **Woman #3** prefers a long-term monogamous relationship that will ultimately lead to marriage, but she is willing to settle for a short-term relationship as long as it is monogamous. Woman #3 will never reveal her true desires and interests easily or straightforwardly.

4) **Woman #4** prefers a long-term monogamous relationship that will ultimately lead to marriage, but she is willing to settle for a weekend fling or a few weeks of enjoyable,

satisfying casual sex. Woman #4 will never reveal her true desires and interests easily or straightforwardly.

5) **Woman #5** (optional) prefers a long-term monogamous relationship that will ultimately lead to marriage, but she is willing engage in any kinky sex act that a man can persuade her to engage in. Woman #5 will never reveal her true desires and interests easily or straightforwardly.

6) **Woman #6** (optional) has no interest in the man (or men) playing the game, but she wants to see if she can get him to offer her a free lunch, a free dinner, a free movie or some other financial-related favor. Woman #6 is going to do her best to pretend like she's interested in having a long-term monogamous relationship with the man (or men) involved in the game for as long as possible.

7) **Woman #7** (optional) has no interest in the man (or men) playing the game, but she wants to see if she can get that man to engage her in a lengthy, entertaining conversation that centers on mutual interests and past experiences. Woman #7 is going to do her best to pretend like she's interested in

having a long-term monogamous relationship with the man (or men) involved in the game for as long as possible.

Once all of the women involved with the game are set, you need to put each woman in a different room. Or at minimum, you need to put the man in one room, and rotate the different women into the room.

The objective of each woman: With the exception of Woman #1, the objective of each woman is to **hold back on revealing what your true underlying desire and interest is**. Secondly, your objective is to engage this man (or men) into as long of a conversation as possible.

The objective of the man (or men): The man will have anywhere from a minimum of forty-five (45) minutes to talk to each of the women, with an absolute maximum of seventy-five (75) minutes of conversation. Someone will have to have a timer or stopwatch.

If the man correctly identifies what woman is Woman #1, what woman is Woman #2, what woman is Woman #3 and so on, he "wins" the game. If at least two or more of his guesses are incorrect, the women win the game. I've done a variation of this game with women, and the women ended up enjoying it almost more than I did.

Again, regardless of who wins the game, the true objective is for the single men to get a better sense of their strengths and weaknesses regarding their interpersonal communication skills with women, and learning how to use their time more efficiently when socializing with women.

Honestly, I don't know if the game would be as fun with one or two women and four-to-seven men, but you can try. Just change up the roles based on my definitions of Reciprocators, Rejecters, and various types of Timewasters.

If you are single man, invite some single females you know to try this game out if they have the free time to do so. You could have three of your male friends and about four-to-seven women.

I guarantee you that you will enjoy yourself! Then mix up the women and the roles and do it all over again.

Have fun . . .

Chapter TWELVE

Upfront and Straightforward

Imagine if a certain percentage of airplane pilots were pretending to be pilots, when in actuality, they were bus drivers. If you had prior knowledge to this phenomenon before boarding a plane, would you feel comfortable knowing your pilot could be a fake?

Imagine if a certain percentage of physicians were pretending to be physicians, when in actuality, they were veterinarians. If you had prior knowledge of this widespread fraud before being admitted into a hospital, would you feel comfortable knowing your physician could be a doctor who specializes in animals?

Imagine if a certain percentage of automotive mechanics were pretending to be auto mechanics, when in actuality they were computer information technology professionals. If you had prior knowledge of this prior to taking your car to the shop for a tune-up and some repairs, would you feel comfortable driving your car afterwards?

If very few of us would feel comfortable sitting on a plane with a suspect pilot, going into surgery with a suspect doctor or driving a car that had been worked on by a suspect mechanic, why should we feel comfortable having intimate sexual relations with someone who might not be who he or she claims to be?

If a man thinks he married an erotically conservative, very prudish "good girl," only later to find out that his wife is a promiscuous whore who has had sex with all of his friends, co-workers and neighbors, do you think he is going to have an easy time getting over being duped? Doubtful. That mutha fu**a might just go out and shoot somebody just for the hell of it.

If a woman thinks she married a good Christian man with good Christian values, only to find out later that he is a pathological liar and a bi-sexual "down low" husband who solicits other men for unprotected sex, do you think she will just forgive him quickly? She might just take a knife and cut his testicles off.

You cannot go around thinking you can play with people's emotions and ego, and that no consequences and/or repercussions are going to come of it. Karma is a bitch. I'm not preaching, I'm just being as real with my knowledge, wisdom and advice as I know how to be.

If you are into casual sex with multiple partners, then you need to be hooking up with men or women who are into the same thing. If you are into crack cocaine, then you need to hook up with members of the opposite sex who are into crack cocaine as well.

The HIV / AIDS virus has not had nearly the negative effect on the dating and relationships arena as frequent lies, deception and manipulative head games have. All of this "pretending" has made some men and women bitter and vindictive, others cynical and wary, and even others mentally ill and emotionally stressed.

Only cowards need to lie about their true desires, interests and intentions. Only those with absolutely no values or principles need to go around misleading people and manipulating people for self-serving motivations. It is time to wake up people.

Forget about the pain and frustration you might be causing others … what about you? If you are busy lying to folk, how do you know you are not dealing with someone more deceptive and manipulative than yourself? You think you are playing her, and in reality, she is playing you. Remember: **Manipulation is always a two-way street**.

When you do right by people, men and women tend to remember you as someone who had a profound impact on their life. When you constantly do wrong by people, you will ultimately lead a lonely and frustrating life. It all catches up to you in the end.

Don't ever think for a moment that reading a dating and relationships book is somehow "trivial." No sir, no mam. Most of us, if not all of us, want someone to spend time with in a romantic and/or sexual manner. Trust me on this. Companionship is always desired.

The desire to hug, kiss and exchange orgasms is just as natural as the desire to sleep, eat food, and drink water or other thirst-quenching liquids. Never allow someone to make you feel guilty for having erotic desires, even if they are "kinky" or unconventional.

As long as you are not a thirty-five year old man trying to have sex with a thirteen or fourteen year old girl, I have no problems with you. As long as you are not a woman having sex with your neighbor's Rottweiler, I have no moral judgments against you.

Kinkiness is highly subjective. My "kinky" could be your "normal" and vice versa. As long as what you are doing in the bedroom (or outside the bedroom) is not illegal, an invasion of someone's physical space, and you are not deceiving them or misleading them in any sort of way, you are good in my book. Live out your lustful desires.

I say, drinks for all of the women ... and blowjobs for all of the men. Okay, maybe not that drunk, fat stinky mutha fu**a over there in the corner talking to himself.

If you are looking for marriage and "Mr. Right" or "Ms. Right," don't try to rush into anything. Take your time. Ask good, straightforward questions. Find out about this person's desires, fears, morals, values, principles and past relationship experiences. Finding out key information is representative of "old school" dating and will do nothing but help you in the long run.

If you are looking for just a one-night stand, weekend fling or other variation of casual sex ... have the cojones to be bold, upfront and straightforward in letting a woman know that. Same goes for the women. In the long-run, you will feel better about yourself and your sense of character and integrity. You will be surprised at the responses you receive.

People come down hard on adult film actors and actresses. Some say porno stars are the scum of the earth. Not hardly. Adult film stars put it all out there. They are not sexually duplicitous and erotically hypocritical like over half of the men and women walking around in society "playing innocent." I respect anyone who puts their sexuality out there for all to see. **Who cares what YOU think about MY sex life.** As far as I know, I am the only one being buried in the coffin.

I hope the contents of these pages help you improve your love life, sex life and overall social life. Everyone deserves to be happy.

I Found Mr. / Ms. Right!! Now What?

Many men say to me, "Hey Alan ... Mode One Behavior helped me identify and eliminate manipulative head games ... I found the woman I want to spend a lot of time with ... but now, do I return to Mode Two Behavior?"

My own brother asked me one time how I felt the Four Modes of Verbal Communication™ fit into the structure and day-to-day interactions between a boyfriend and girlfriend, an engaged couple, and/or a husband and wife.

Expressing yourself in a highly self-assured, upfront and straightforwardly honest manner becomes even more important within the context of a long-term relationship. Once you start suppressing your real feelings with your romantic companion, your relationship is doomed.

Who could ever maintain an enjoyable, successful relationship if there are 'skeletons in the closet' (i.e., closely guarded secrets) and/or pent-up frustrations and camouflaged resentment and bitterness?

One thing Yours Truly cannot do is have a "relationship of convenience." What is the point? I have had many women make comments to me such as, "I knew the day I married my ex-husband that I did not truly love him." Then why in the hell did you marry him? "I knew within a week after I married my wife that I wasn't going to stop seeing other women . . ." Then why would you pretend to be enthusiastic about monogamy? Makes no sense to me.

No one in life "forces" you to enter into any romantic relationship. There was a time decades ago when you had the infamous "shotgun wedding" if you accidently got a woman pregnant and her father wanted you to 'make an honest woman out of her,' but that out-of-date scenario aside, why would anyone ever enter into a long-term relationship under the pretense of monogamy if you know deep-down that is not what you want? Fear + Spoiled Ego = Desire to Manipulate.

I had an ex-girlfriend of mine confess to me that the main reason she married her now husband was for financial security. It would be different if this guy was a self-made millionaire with a revenue stream that was never going to stop. Then, I might halfway give her a pass. Her husband is a 9-to-5 hard-working man like any other guy in society. He could lose his job any day of any week. Then where would her 'financial security' come from?

Knowing what role you play in a relationship also helps. Why are good football teams successful? Because you have **specifically defined roles**. You don't have three quarterbacks on the field at the same time. You don't have running backs trying to play the role of the offensive linemen and wide receivers delivering the ball to the quarterback at the center position. Team players know their role.

The United States of America does not have two Presidents, nor does any major city have two Mayors or any state in this country have two Governors. In government, the power to make important decisions usually comes from **one person**.

It cracks me up when I hear women say, *"Why does my husband have to be in charge? Why can't we both be in charge of the relationship?"* Because that relationship will never work. Either the man needs to be in charge, or if he's willing to defer to his wife, then let her run the relationship. But this notion of "I have 50% of the decision-making power and my spouse has 50% of the decision-making power in the relationship" is crap. Someone has to captain the ship. Two people can both have power in different areas, but ultimately, there has to be **one** final decision-maker.

Know your role. Be hardline against manipulative behavior by your spouse or loved one that goes against your morals, values and principles. Write down on paper whose role it is to spend most of the weekday evenings with the kid(s), whose role it is to pay most of the bills, whose role it is to keep what room of the house clean, and so on and so on.

You know what's funny? People always criticize men who are "pimps" and the relationship they have with their "whores." They say that this sort of relationship between a man and a woman is chauvinistic, sexist, shallow, misogynistic and disrespectful to women. What boggles my mind is, if the relationship is so bad … why does the typical pimp have more than his share of women?

The pimp knows his role. The whore knows her role. And you know what? The relationship works. I'm not encouraging men and women to go out and develop a pimp-whore relationship after reading this, but I'm just pointing out that when you know your role in a relationship, it works.

That's why sometimes a married man can have a long-lasting relationship with a mistress that will almost seem better than the relationship that married man has with his wife. Now before you have a hissy fit, I am not condoning adultery. Not in any way, shape or form. I think adultery is a cowardly act of infidelity.

The reality is the married man knows his role and so does his mistress. Some husbands and wives do not know their roles.

FOR A RELATIONSHIP TO LAST INDEFINITELY, YOU MUST HAVE SPECIFICALLY DEFINED ROLES IN THAT RELATIONSHIP.

Be brutally honest with your partner to the point of possibly hurting their feelings or bruising their ego. The pain is usually short-lived, and will go away soon. The pain of being lied to or mislead last for a long, long, long time. Trust me on that.

I hear people say, "I believe compromise is the #1 factor that contributes to a great relationship." More invalid crap. I am not compromising my desires for any woman. Instead of compromising, what you need to do is find someone with many of the same interests as yourself. That works better than compromising.

I love chicken wings. I mean, I really, really love chicken wings (chicken wings are like the food equivalent to crack cocaine for me). Now, if I met a woman who said, *"Alan ... I want you to eat chicken wings ever other Friday, and we're going to eat fish or lasagna on the other Fridays,"* I would be showing that woman the exit door.

I'm going to eat my doggone chicken wings when I want to. I'm not changing or modifying my behavior to please, impress or accommodate any woman. All that does is lead to suppressed bitterness and resentment towards a woman when or if things go wrong later on. I see this sort of scenario play out in long-term relationships all of the time.

Let's break down the Four Modes of Verbal Communication™ in this manner for long-term relationships:

_____

Mode One attitude: My Romantic Partner and I share a lot of the same interests, and we tolerate the differences between us.

_____

Mode Two attitude: My Romantic Partner and I sacrifice many of our own interests in order to please each other, and we compromise on our differences.

_____

Mode Three attitude: I am my partner's "bitch." Everything they say goes. I don't have a say in the relationship. I just do whatever I am told. Even if I don't like it.

_____

Mode Four attitude: I can't stand the sight of my romantic partner. I have no idea why I am still with this mutha fu**a. He/She gets on my last nerve. We haven't had sex in weeks, if not months.

UPFRONT and STRAIGHTFORWARD

What is your romantic relationship? Mode One? Mode Two? Mode Three? Mode Four? I hope it's not either of the latter two (unless you are a masochist, then Mode Three works for you).

DON'T COMPROMISE YOUR DESIRES AND INTERESTS TO ACCOMMODATE OTHERS; INSTEAD, FIND SOMEONE WHO HAS MANY DESIRES AND INTERESTS WHICH ARE SIMILAR TO YOURS.

Everyone who has read my book knows how I feel about subjective criticisms. I think you should allow them to go in one ear and out the other. They have no place in long-term romantic relationships.

"You eat too fast!" So.
"You talk too much!" So.
"You dress too provocatively!" So.
"You use too much profanity!" So.
"You want to have sex too much!" Uhm . . . . so.

Unless a man or woman signed a "contract" of sorts, and they specifically listed on this mutually agreed upon document that they would never eat too fast, talk too much, dress too provocatively, use too much profanity, or express too much interest in sex ... then all of these are subjective criticisms.

In other words, they are based on **your own opinion**. When a man and a woman are in a long-term relationship, it is not their obligation to live up to **your standards**. I would never enter into any long-term relationship in order to live up to a woman's standards and expectations. I live by my own standards, and I look for women who happen to enjoy those standards.

No corporation in America could get away with that unless they put it in writing. You notice how when you get hired for just about any job, they provide you with an "Employee Manual?" This is to let you know what they expect of you. They are communicating to you their expectations and desired standards for your behavior.

Have you ever had a wife or husband hand you such a document? The "This is what I expect of you as my wife / husband" manual? "This is what I expect of you as my girlfriend / boyfriend" manual?

Once someone agrees to behavior on paper, it then becomes objective. I have no problem with mutually agreed upon objective criticisms. If I made a vow to be faithful to you, and I break that vow, you have all the right in the world to harshly criticize me. That is an objective criticism.

But I made no vow to eat chicken wings only two Fridays per month. If you tell me, *"Alan, you eat chicken wings too much!"* I'm going to look you in your eyes, smirk, and calmly say, "So."

HARSH, SUBJECTIVE CRITICISMS ARE VASTLY OVERRATED AND FOR THE MOST PART, UNNECESSARY. ONLY CONCENTRATE ON EXPRESSING OBJECTIVE CRITICISMS OF YOUR PARTNER'S BEHAVIOR.

It amazes me how many people let themselves go once they feel secure in a long-term relationship. Can you imagine if you purchased a nice, shiny, Porsche 911 and then once you signed all of the contracts and paid your first few car notes, all of the sudden the color started fading and the finish on your car just looked jacked up?

Why do men and women feel like they can get married and then just gain forty, fifty or sixty plus pounds? What the hell? Keep your body in shape. You don't have to be a serious gym rat, or exercise like you're trying to win a beauty pageant or fitness contest, but c'mon men and women ... no one wants you gaining weight in the relationship for no reason.

So you are a woman and you just gave birth to three children in five years? Okay, you have an excuse for letting yourself go a wee bit.

Even then though, purchase a stationary bicycle or inexpensive treadmill. You might fool yourself into believing that your partner loves having sex with you because of your great personality and intelligence, but the reality is, he loved that nice butt of yours and she loved your six-pack abs.

AN EMPHASIS ON HEALTH AND FITNESS KEEPS THE EROTIC SPARKS IN A RELATIONSHIP INDEFINITELY

Okay, that's about all of the advice I have to offer regarding long-term relationships, and how the Four Modes of Verbal Communication™ and other factors come into play.

Upfront, straightforward honesty is not something you just practice until you find Ms. Right. You incorporate that characteristic into your day-to-day, week-to-week, month-to-month, year-to-year behavior.

You can never go wrong with real, raw truth. "Pleasant Lies" (which at one time was going to be the alternative title to this book) will always do you in eventually. Lies mask the problem; Truth solves the problem.

Don't enter into a romantic relationship in order to become happy. Develop a sense of happiness even before you meet a life-long romantic companion. Then, once you have developed a boat load of happiness ... share that happiness with whomever you meet.

Peace, Love and Happiness to you all.

Mode One Baby . . . make it happen.

Alan Roger Currie was born in Gary, Indiana and is the author of the popular paperback, *Mode One: Let the Women Know What You're REALLY Thinking*. Currie graduated from Indiana University in Bloomington, Indiana with a degree in Economics and a minor in Theatre and Drama.

Currie has previously pursued an acting career, acting on stage in college and acting in local, regional and national television commercials. Currie was also the 1989 Grand Prize Winner of the Chicago Miller Lite Beer Stand-Up Comedy Search Contest, the same contest which the late Bernie Mac won one year later. Currie has also pursued a career as a screenwriter and filmmaker, and has written and directed two short films.

Currie is the host of his own talk radio show entitled *Upfront and Straightforward with Alan Roger Currie* and has been featured in *Essence* magazine and on *The Morning Show with Mike and Juliet* television talk show, among other media appearances. Currie resides in Northwest Indiana.

CPSIA information can be obtained
at www.ICGtesting.com
Printed in the USA
BVHW070319040419
544581BV00002B/194/P

9 781601 457950